MW01088329

A Skeptic Challenges a Christian

An honest conversation about reasons to believe

David W. Pendergrass, PhD

Perspicacious Publishing

Houston

Contents

David W. Pendergrass received his Bachelor of Arts in Religious Studies from Gardner-Webb University (NC), his Master of Divinity in Pastoral Studies from the School of Divinity at Gardner-Webb University, and his Doctorate of Philosophy in Historical Theology from Baylor University (TX). He is an ordained minister and the founding pastor of The Disciple Church in Houston, TX (Thedisciplechurch.org). He also serves on the Bible faculty at Houston Christian High School in Houston, TX. David is married to Elaine and has two children.

A Word of Gratitude

I wish to express my gratitude to my colleagues in the Bible faculty at Houston Christian High School for their helpful input concerning my manuscript. I also thank my students as HC for their incessant need for clarity and concision. They are the inspiration for this manuscript. I also thank Kevin Sivils for his incredibly helpful information regarding publishing. He was always ready to help. Finally, I thank my wife for her careful reading and insightful questions. She is a constant source of encouragement.

κύριον δὲ τὸν Χριστὸν ἁγιάσατε ἐν ταῖς καρδίαις ὑμῶν,
ἕτοιμοι ἀεὶ πρὸς ἀπολογίαν παντὶ τῷ αἰτοῦντι ὑμᾶς
λόγον περὶ τῆς ἐν ὑμῖν ἐλπίδος,

1 Peter 3:15

To

skeptics like me

Preface

I'm very skeptical. I'm not really a *skeptic*, since that would mean that I haven't made up my mind. I have; I'm a Christian. Yet, it takes me a long time to believe something. I ask a lot of questions. I need things to make sense, especially when it comes to belief in God or any religion. My journey to and through Christianity has been driven by a constant desire to know if Christianity is really *true*—not just a person's opinion or preference—but *true*. So, I like skeptics. I can relate to them.

Skeptics who have made up their mind against believing in God are called atheists. Atheists have been attacking Christianity since the inception of Christianity. This means that Christians have been defending attacks for over two thousand years. Recently, there has been a *massive* foment of atheist works, such as Richard Dawkins, *The God Delusion*; Christopher Hitchens, *God is not Great: How Religion Poisons Everything*; Sam Harris, *Letter to a Christian Nation*; or Victor Stenger: *The New Atheism: Taking a Stand for Science and Reason*. One can simply type "atheism" on Amazon.com to see the overwhelming amount of literature being produced on the topic. It must be said that these authors are not all the same: they have different "bones to pick," different writing styles, and vastly different fields of specialty (most of whom have no or very little training in Christianity or philosophy). Caricatures of Christianity abound. While reading some of these works, you might be reminded of C.S. Lewis' critique of certain atheists in his time: "Such people put up a version of Christianity suitable for a child of six and make that the object of their attack."[1]

Against their desire, these outspoken atheists have been labeled "new" because they differ from previous generations of atheists. Previous attempts to rebut Christianity by atheists primarily (but not only) occurred in philosophy departments at universities and in the publication of unpopular books. Moreover, their critique was primarily (though certainly not exclusively) reserved to *philosophical* arguments (one thinks of Antony Flew).

This new generation of atheists is both the same and different from their predecessors. Their primary complaints are not new at all: science is the only true mode of knowledge; believing in God is driven by neurosis, wishfulfillment, or evolutionary needs; belief in God is for stupid people; you can be moral without God. Yet, atheists these days are debating in the public square like never before, they are writing popular books that top best-selling lists, and they are most certainly *not* relegating their debates to philosophical arguments. They can be crass and unrelentingly opposed to all forms of religion. The gloves are off. Religion is poisonous and causes all the wars; it is for the stupid, moronic, delusional, and fairytale-hungry people who are scared of the unknown. Belief in God stifles every kind of scientific and social progress, and any respect given to religion must be dismissed as the "growing pains" of our version of primates, *homo sapiens*.

Remember, most of the vitriol from the new atheists can be attributed to their view that believing in God is like believing in the tooth fairy. How would you feel toward such people? Really, imagine a person who vigorously believes in the tooth fairy. You might feel sympathy for the person at first. Maybe they were really unintelligent (i.e., too stupid to know the difference) or forced to believe it because of their family or environment. But eventually, having to debate "tooth-fairyists" would just frustrate you, especially if you were intellectually arrogant. You would find it profoundly odd that they would gather together each week to sing songs to the tooth fairy and talk to the tooth fairy. On top of that, imagine that you believe tooth-fairyists are dangerous and wicked and cause all the wars.

Just know that for most atheists, if you believe in God, talking with you is at least as frustrating as having to talk with a tooth-fairyist. A warmongering, delusional, hypocritical, brainwashed, tooth-fairyist: that's what you are in their view. Sure, you might meet some nice tooth-fairyists now and then, but on the whole, they are to be avoided at all costs, and certainly no respect should be given to them.

Well, tooth-fairyists, especially the Christian kind, have never been silent. Literature is being published every year that is added to the hundreds of apologetics books that already exist. I have been influenced by several of the great, recent books that have been offered as responses to this "new atheism." Here is a very small sample of the fine material that has been released in the last few years:

William Lane Craig, *Reasonable Faith*, 3rd Ed. (Crossway, 2008)

_____, *On Guard: Defending Your Faith with Reason and Precision* (David C. Cook, 2010)

William Lane Craig and Chad Meister, *God is Great, God is Good: Why Believing in God is Reasonable and Responsible* (IVP, 2009)

Norman Geisler and Frank Turek, *I Don't Have Enough Faith to be an Atheist* (Crossway, 2004)

Norman Geisler and Paul Hoffman, eds., *Why I Am a Christian: Leading Thinkers Explain Why They Believe* (Baker, 2006)

Paul Copan and William Lane Craig, eds., *Contending with Christianity's Critics* (B&H Academic, 2009)

Paul Copan, *Is God a Moral Monster?* (Baker, 2011)

Alister McGrath, *The Passionate Intellect* (IVP, 2010)

John Lennox, *God's Undertaker: Has Science Buried God?* (Lion UK, 2009)

_____, *Stephen Hawking and God: Whose Design is it Anyway?* (Lion US, 2011)

_____, *Gunning for God: A Critique of the New Atheism* (Lion UK, 2011).

I must mention that a whole host of books and essays written by C.S. Lewis are essential. Of course, they were not written in response to the "new atheists" of our generation, but written to counter atheism in his own day (ca. sixty years ago). Nevertheless, his writings are as relevant as ever. It is striking evidence of how familiar the arguments of these "new atheists" are, when one reads sixty-year-old essays that could have been written a week ago to counter any number of modern-day atheists. This is great news: you could hardly find a better guide to Christian apologetics than C.S. Lewis. No writing outside the Bible has influenced my thinking like the writings of C.S. Lewis. I would read everything you could find that's published with his name on it (e.g., *Mere Christianity*, *Miracles*, *God in the Dock*, or *The World's Last Night and Other Essays*).

Also, I highly recommend William Lane Craig's website (Reasonablefaith.org) and Greg Koukl's website and organization, Stand to Reason (Str.org). Finally, the Fixed Point Foundation (Fixed-point.org) has produced several outstanding debates available on DVD that are well worth your time.

It will be helpful to say a word about what this book is and is not. First, this book is not written for the specialist. In fact, if you have extensive knowledge in philosophy or Christianity, this book probably won't be very interesting to you. Second, this book is not a formal rebuttal of any one book or idea. Finally, this book is not exhaustive: every possible rejoinder or argument is not tendered. Such a book would require thousands of pages.

So why do we need another book? Perhaps we don't. There are already copious works available. Yet, I think there's a need to continue this discussion concerning God's existence and the truth claims of Christianity. *I hope this book serves as a supplement to the material that already exists by providing a synthetic, conversational overview of several key challenges to belief in God and Christianity.* I still have unanswered questions myself. However, this book represents in a nutshell why I, as a practicing Christian, think Christianity is the most rationally and emotionally satisfying option available to humans among the world's religions.

A word about the format and style of this book: I've deliberately kept technical jargon to a minimum (unless I define it), including the common "Christianese" of evangelical Christians. It usually takes *me* some time to translate common Christian expressions; I can't imagine how obscure they must sound to nonbelievers. In addition, I want this to read like a conversation. This is the reason why I use contractions. Since I tend to emphasize certain words or expressions when I'm talking, I've tried to demonstrate that by italicizing. Also, in case this book will be used in a small group format, I have included some reflection questions for each chapter at the end of the book. Finally, you might notice that I spend more time on arguing for God's existence than for particular truth claims of Christianity. This is deliberate. Most skeptics in my experience have bigger hurdles believing in a Creator God in general, than in believing in Christianity in particular.

Finally, I like *to talk* about religion. In fact, I find that dialogues are very enjoyable and helpful because of the give-and-take. If I could sit together with you one afternoon and have a conversation about God and Christianity over a very cold Coke Zero, what would it sound like?

Perhaps something like this.

David W. Pendergrass
Season of Advent, 2011

CHAPTER ONE

Are you really open-minded?

"Excuse me. I couldn't help but see that book you were reading."

Oh yeah? It's great. It's by a well-respected New Testament scholar, N.T. Wright. It's called *The Challenge of Jesus*. I can't recommend his works enough.

"So . . . you actually believe in all that?"

Hi, I'm David.

"Oh, hello. I'm Every-skeptic-you've-ever-met-and-read-and-heard-about."

Nice to meet you.

"So, you believe in all that?"

All what?

"You know . . . God and whatever. You actually believe in all that?"

Only on Tuesdays.

[Looks confused.]

Just messing with you. Yes; I do believe in all that. I'm a Christian, if that's what you mean: a disciple or student of Jesus of Nazareth. Yes, I do believe in God and I believe that Christianity is true.

"Why?"

There's a whole bunch of reasons, really. But the thing that matters the most to me is—and I know this might sound strange or cheesy—my relationship with Jesus of Nazareth. Jesus has changed my life.

"Yeah, I respect all kinds of great moral teachers. They have had a big impact on me too."

Huh. That's good, I guess. Except I don't just follow Jesus' teachings because of some historical impact He had. I actually believe that Jesus is not dead. I'm convinced He's alive, right now. I pray to a living person who actually listens to me. I sing songs to a person who is listening. Whenever I serve others, I . . .

"Yeah, but couldn't you be delusional?"

Of course.

"What?!"

Of course I must concede that it's possible. You might not exist. I could be dreaming or delusional about you, too.

"Well, *I* think I exist."

[Smiling] Of course you do.

"But that's different. What makes you so certain you talk to this 'Jesus'?"

Several things. There's not just one thing that convinces me, but a whole host of . . .

"So, you don't ever doubt?"

Doubt? Of course . . . but not often. I also sometimes doubt whether or not my wife loves me or if my friends like me or if people can be trusted or . . .

"So, if you doubt, then why believe it?"

Because I'm scared of the dark.

"Oh . . ." [Looks serious.]

I'm just kidding. That's a common expression by some popular atheists: they accuse us of being "scared of the dark." First, I believe in God because believing in a Creator God makes the most sense of multiple things, like the origin of the universe, the origin of multiple constants throughout the universe, the origin of life, the origin of the soul, and the origin of morality. That is, there are certain scientific facts that point to the existence of a Creator God.[1]

But, my faith isn't in science. Scientific facts aren't enough to convince me that . . .

"But science has solved all that."

Woah. Well, I really disagree. And I'll be happy to chat about it if you'd like.

"OK, well, there are still questions. But why can't you just say that we don't know? That's what scientists do: they are comfortable with saying, 'I don't know. And one day we'll figure it out.' Why are you Christians so quick to bring in some outside fairy tale to solve this? It seems so lazy."

Of course I could just say, "I don't know." Of course I could. And there's a whole host of things about which I *do* say, "I don't know." That is, I don't believe God is a scientific explanation for every phenomenon in the universe.

For example, scientists are certain that the universe is expanding. In fact, it's speeding up as it expands. Why? Scientists are not absolutely certain, though the current suggestion that is gaining consensus is hypothetical "dark matter" and "dark energy" (these are said to constitute about 98% of the universe). Now, I don't know if dark matter and dark energy exist since there is no absolute, definitive evidence yet. But what I don't do is say that because scientists don't know why it's expanding, it must be God. I don't throw in "God" every time I don't understand why something is happening in the universe. There are plenty of facts about the universe that we don't understand now that we one day we will understand.

Yet, there are certain scientific facts which raise special questions. The *nature of these facts or questions* suggests that they exist because a personal Agent caused or causes them. But, I'd like to talk about that later if we get to it.

But to finish, the second and main reason I'm a Christian is because Christianity has the most historical evidence, which means I believe Christianity's particular truth claims are true. And if Christianity is true, then God certainly exists.

Third, I'm a Christian because I have had profound religious experiences with the living Spirit of Jesus.

"Huh. Well, I believe in science."

That's an interesting way to put it.

"Put what?"

That you believe *in* science, as if science were a person in whom you could put your trust. I believe *in* my wife or my friends, but I wouldn't say that I believe *in* the laws of mathematics. I believe *that* science can help us know certain types of truth, but I don't believe *in* science.

"Well, I mean that I believe in the fact that science can prove everything about existence. I just believe in things that I can see or can be proven."

I don't think you really mean that.

"Huh?"

So you don't believe in justice and fairness and beauty and love?

"Sure."

Why? You said you only believe in things you can see. What does justice look like?

"Well, I could never believe in some imaginary Santa Claus in the sky, or, since you apparently believe in the Old Testament, a hateful, racist, warmongering tyrant in the sky."

[Looks serious.] You don't believe in Santa?
Hey, I absolutely concur! Besides your faulty understanding of God in the Old Testament, I could never believe in Santa Claus in the sky or a Tyrant-in-the-Sky.

"That's what you believe, isn't it?"

It might be best to *ask* me what I believe, rather than assume it. I tell you what: I won't assume I know what *you* believe and why, if you won't assume you know what *I* believe and why.

"Fair enough. Then why do you believe in God?"

Well, that depends on what kind of god, or which god, you're talking about. I don't believe in the pantheist *god* of Hinduism, *Brahman* (where the universe is deity), or the *life-force*, *chi*. There are numerous gods I don't believe in. I've never believed in the Japanese sun-goddess, Amaterasu, the Egyptian god, Ra', the Greek god, Zeus, the Chinese god, Shangdi, and none of the Hindu gods, such as Vishnu, Ganesh, or Sakti, and on and on down the Pantheon list we could go.

"So, why don't you believe in them?"

I would be willing to be convinced that they exist, either from logical proofs or compelling historical evidence. Yet, since (1) I do not w of any compelling evidence of their existence; (2) I believe Christianity has the most compelling truth claims; and (3) Christianity does not consider any other gods to exist, I do not believe those other gods exist.

"OK. So you *do* believe in the Christian god. Why? I don't know of any evidence that your god exists."

Some evidence of God is circumstantial, or implicit, like footprints on the sand serve as evidence that someone has walked there before. Other evidence is based on historical records. Before I go into too much detail, I must make this crucial point.

I also don't believe in leprechauns. I don't believe in unicorns. I don't believe in fairies. However, *and I must be clear*, I'm not an *a*leprechaunist. I'm not an *a*unicornist. I'm not an *a*fairiest. That is, I am not convinced that they do *not exist*. Rather, I am agnostic, that is, ignorant, of their existence. I am really, genuinely, open to their existence. Not only am I open to their existence, these creatures may exist. They really might. Who knows? Perhaps they used to exist in some remote part of the Earth, died off, and then lived on in legends. Or perhaps we'll discover creatures like them in some remote part of the galaxy on a distant planet.

Nevertheless, what I certainly don't do is rule out their existence without any reason because I don't like the idea of them existing. I have no emotional, psychological, or moral reason to disbelieve in their existence. I have no reason to look for reasons for them not to exist. In fact, if someone told me that fairies were more authoritative than I, and that one day a fairy will hold me accountable to everything I did and said in this life, I would most certainly be interested in its existence.

The question that matters the most before we ever begin the discussion of fairies and leprechauns or Zeus or Vishnu must be: Am I *open to the possibility that there might be actual evidence of their existence? Am I really open to that possibility?*

"Well, it's Christians who are close-minded; enslaved, really. You believe what you believe because you're afraid you'll go to hell, right? In other words, there is no way that you're open-minded if you're terrified of going to hell."

Again, it's best to ask me what I believe, rather than assuming it. And to answer your question: no. I'm not a Christian because I'm afraid of going to hell.

I know that most atheist heroes these days, like Dawkins and Hitchens, are begging their audiences to be "set free" from the shackles of fear; it's just that I don't know of any Christian who is a Christian because of fear. I bet they exist somewhere in the world, but nevertheless, I'm not a Christian because of a fear of death or of hell.

"Most Christians I've met seem like they've been brainwashed. They just seem so weird."

Yeah, I've met some weird ones myself. But, I can't speak for all or most Christians. I can speak for myself. I am not brainwashed in a cult. I don't believe in Jesus to have "fire insurance" (i.e., a pass not to go to hell). I don't believe in Jesus to appease my parents or peers. I don't believe in Jesus because I live in America.

[Looks doubtful.] "OK."

To be clear about those things I don't believe in, like Zeus or unicorns, so far, I haven't heard anyone make a compelling case. This is why I don't believe in them: not because I've ruled their existence *before we've begun*, or because I've heard arguments that are contradictory, or because I've been presented any evidence that is tenuous and uncorroborated. Rather, no one has presented any type of evidence at all. Nevertheless, I'm still quite open to their existence. In fact, I think it'd be pretty cool if they did exist.

"OK."

7

My point is: I'd love to have a conversation about God with you. But, I just don't want to waste my time. If you're really willing to discuss this with me, I'd be happy to. However, if you've already made up your mind that there is no way that God exists—and I respect that decision—then there's no reason to continue. I need to know that you're really open-minded to the *possibility* that God exists. If not, you'll dismiss any kind of evidence I give you.

"Honestly, I'm not *that* open-minded to it. I've just never heard any compelling reason to believe in a god. I would need extraordinary evidence to believe in such a thing."

Honestly, I don't know what "extraordinary evidence" would look like or mean.

If you're not open-minded at all then nothing I will ever say will convince you. Here's an analogy.

I have a brother named Stephen. We grew up together. He also has red hair, and looks like my mom's side of the family.

If Joe the "*abrotherist*" (someone who didn't believe brothers exist) were to come up to me and say, 'I know that your brother doesn't exist, so prove to me he exists.' I would certainly feel like the conversation is being sabotaged. I'd feel that our conversation would be pointless because he would not listen to any evidence I'd offer.

"Yeah, I can see that."

It'd go something like this:

DP: "Well, my brother's name is Stephen. Here's tons of pictures of him."

Joe: "I can do the same thing in Photoshop. You could say that those are all fakes. Or, you probably just got those from Google Images."

DP: "But I'm in the photos too—see me right here, and here, and in this one?"

Joe: "Google Images. I can find people who look like you too on the Internet."

DP: "OK. Here is his license and birth certificate."

Joe: "What?! You could say that those are all forged. I can make you a license right now and forge tons of birth certificates. Or, at least, I could get someone to do it for me."

DP: "Hmm. Well, here is his hair sample and blood sample."

Joe: "You could say that you got that from a homeless person a few minutes ago."

DP: "Well, I'm running out of things I would consider evidence."

Joe: "Figures. All you 'believe-in-a-brother types' are all the same! All I ask for is simple evidence and you can't do it. Tell you what: I'll believe you have a brother if you can make him appear right now."

DP: "Uhhh . . . I'm sorry; this is impossible. He has a free will and lives down the road a bit. He doesn't move at my bidding. I'm not sure if he's available or if he even wants to come to . . ."

Joe: "I knew it! All I asked is for one simple thing! Just have your brother appear right now. What's the big deal? Or, I tell you what, just get your brother to send you a text message right now and con-firm he's your brother."

DP: "OK. Give me some time." (I type on my phone and wait). "Here it is! Look."

Joe: "That could be anyone, how do I know that's your brother?"

DP: "Alright, let me see if I can get him. (I return back within an hour). Here! Let me introduce you to my brother, Stephen."

Joe: "Yeah right. This could be anyone. You could say that this is that homeless guy who gave you the hair samples and blood types."

DP: "Wait a second. Ask my brother about my childhood and see if our stories coincide."

Joe: "This doesn't prove anything. You could say that you've spent the last hour going over stories in collusion. Anyone can make up stories and agree."

[Laughing] "But I would never do that. No one is that close-minded."

Yes they most certainly are, my friend. A favorite phrase of someone who *already* doesn't believe is "you could say . . .," with no evidence for that theory or story. I have found it overwhelmingly common that this one phrase is a ploy. It's a red herring. It's meant to get the discussion off track and waste time at best, or at worst, embarrass the person.

"Are you scared of alternate theories? Is that why you believe in God? Because you've never listened to alternate theories?"

Of course not. I am open to alternate theories in any field of knowledge. I just want to draw attention to the fact that if you find yourself offering tons of alternate theories or stories with no evidence of that alternate story, it demonstrates you're not open to being convinced. Remember, a theory or story is not evidence. They are not proofs. They are just stories. I will be interested to see in our conversation how often you use that phrase. Every atheist I've ever met counters every single belief, like with my brother's existence, with an alternate story, and thinks this just settles the issue. Remember, a probable explanation is not rendered useless just because you can come up with any other conceivable story of why something happened.

"Yeah, but I don't know of any serious scientist or thinker who rules out God's existence before the conversation. They just let the evidence lead them to their conclusion."

I must disagree. Scientists do not always come to their conclusions based solely on the evidence. Their worldview often guides their conclusions.

Here is a perfect example. This is a widespread quote by retired Professor of Zoology and Biology at Harvard University, Richard Lewontin. "Our willingness to accept scientific claims that are *against common sense* is the key to an understanding of the real struggle between science and the supernatural. We take the side of science in spite of the *patent absurdity* of some of its constructs, in spite of its *failures to fulfill many of its extravagant promises* of health and life, in spite of the tolerance of the scientific community for *unsubstantiated just-so stories*, because we have a prior commitment to *materialism*. It is not that the methods and institutions of science somehow compel us to accept a material explanation of the phenomenal world but, on the contrary, that we are *forced* by our *a priori* adherence to *material causes* to create an apparatus of investigation and a set of concepts that produce material explanations, no matter how *counterintuitive*, no matter how mystifying to the uninitiated. Moreover that materialism is absolute *for we cannot allow a divine foot in the door.* . . . To appeal to an omnipotent deity is to allow that at any moment the regularities of nature may be ruptured, that miracles may happen."[2]

Now, at least he's honest. Dr. Lewontin has let the world know that he and his peers are *materialists*. It's astonishing that Dr. Lewontin says that the key to being a good scientist is to believe in things that are "against common sense," "patently absurd," "unsubstantiated just-so stories," and "counterintuitive." And Theists are called crazy! If he's the pinnacle of open-mindedness, then I'm happy to be called "close-minded."

I'm glad there are countless scientists who actually are led by any form of evidence, not pinned down by prior commitments to a worldview.

Francis Collins, considered one of the most distinguished

geneticists of our time, is a former-atheist-turned-Christian. He was the former Head of the Human Genome project, and is currently the director of the U.S. Department of Health & Human Services' National Institutes of Health. He is responsible for the team that mapped the eight-point-one billion character code which is the human genome. I appreciate what he says about his initial considerations of Christianity. When an old Christian woman at a hospital asked him what he believed, he said, "I'm not really sure." He continues:

"That moment haunted me for several days. Did I not consider myself a scientist? Does a scientist draw conclusions without considering the data? Could there be a more important question in all of human existence than 'Is there a God?' And yet there I found myself, with combination of willful blindness and something that could only be properly described as arrogance, having avoided any serious consideration that God might be a real possibility. Suddenly all my arguments seemed very thin, and I had the sensation that the ice under my feet was cracking. . . . I determined to have a look at the facts, no matter what the outcome."[3]

I appreciate that he was open-minded.

This reminds me of something else Collins said once. Collins debated evolutionary biologist and outspoken atheist, Richard Dawkins in 2006. Dawkins got angry when Collins suggested that the Christian God has no creator. (Dawkins cannot tolerate any explanation that does not have another materialistic explanation.)

Collins' response was appropriate: "I do object to the assumption that anything that might be outside of nature is ruled out of the conversation. That's an impoverished view of the kinds of questions we humans can ask, such as "Why am I here?", "What happens after we die?", "Is there a God?" If you refuse to acknowledge their appropriateness, you end up with a zero probability of God after examining the natural world because it doesn't convince you on a proof basis. But if your mind is open about whether God might exist, you can point to aspects of the universe that are consistent with that conclusion."[4]

"Huh."

To be open-minded means seeking earnestly for answers. Christians have never had problems with questioning and wanting to understand. Even though we don't have all the answers, we're certainly interested in finding answers. It reminds me of something one of the greatest thinkers in the West, St. Augustine, said concerning interpreting the biblical book of Genesis. "The fact is, you see, people who have a genuine religious interest in learning put far more questions about this text than these irreligious wretches (here he's referencing thinkers in an ancient philosophy called "Manichaeism"); *but the difference between them is that the former seek in order to find, while the latter are at no pains at all to do anything except not to find what they are seeking.*"[5]

"What's your point?"

Perhaps the most difficult question to ask yourself concerning God's existence is, "Am I genuinely open to the possibility that God exists?" Or as Augustine said, are you really "seeking to find?"

\

CHAPTER TWO

It's all about your worldview

"I guess I'm open to it. But, why would all those scientists rule out God's existence? They must know something you don't."

Worldview. It's about your worldview. And by worldview, I mean the way you see and understand reality. There's more to it than that but that's all I'm emphasizing right now: *how you see reality*. For example, if you believe that the universe is all there is, then there is no possible way for God to exist. This would make you a Materialist or Naturalist (being a *materialist* is not the same as being *materialistic* or greedy).

Carl Sagan, former astrophysicist, astronomer, and cosmologist, said the very popular quote any scientist knows: "The cosmos is all that is or ever was or ever will be." This is materialism or naturalism.

And please make no mistake: this is an *a priori*, or predetermined, belief about reality. That is, a person does *not* come to this worldview because of scientific evidence. Science simply cannot demonstrate that *all* that exists is matter and energy.

And perhaps most important to remember, one's worldview *greatly* determines how you view the evidence.

Most materialists/naturalists also believe in a particular form of arriving at knowledge. They typically say that all real or trustworthy knowledge comes from the scientific method. That is, if what you're saying can't be verified by empirical observation (either now or in the future), then it can't be known. On a popular level, this is called "scientism." Philosophically, this is called Logical Positivism (or Verificationism).

Now this is fine to believe unless there is something that makes materialism and/or scientism false. And therein lays the problem: there are fundamental flaws with the worldview of materialism and the methodological assumptions of scientism, which make them both logically incoherent. We can talk about them if you'd like.

"No, no. That's not true. Scientists use all kinds of methodologies to test their hypotheses."

That's partly true, but the *dominant* belief among those of us in the Western world is that humans discover truth, or come to know something, through the methods of science. This is spread throughout the scientific literature. For example, Dr. Peter Atkins, Professor of Chemistry (and outspoken atheist) at Oxford has said, "There is no reason to suppose that science cannot deal with every aspect of existence."[1] This is scientism (or Logical Positivism or Verificationism).

Bertrand Russell, one of the well-known atheists in the mid-20th cent., said, "Whatever knowledge is attainable, must be attained by scientific methods; and what science cannot discover mankind cannot know."[2] This is scientism (or Logical Positivism or Verificationism).

Logical Positivism (or Verificationism), which had its heyday in the 1920s and 30s, is the philosophical view which asserts that statements which have no scientific evidence to corroborate the statement are meaningless statements. It's literally speaking gibberish if there is no scientific proof. Stating, "there is a God" or "I love you" is like saying, "bloppty blah blah" because it's all meaningless without scientific proof.

Logical Positivism has been absolutely abandoned for varied reasons by philosophers since the 1950s. In other words, no philosopher in scholarship actually holds this view anymore because Logical Positivism has been demonstrated to be certainly false. The chief problem being, the whole system is self-refuting. The statement "all that exists is proven by science" cannot be demonstrated scientifically. Saying, "all that exists is proven by science" is like saying "bloppty blah blah" because there is no scientific evidence for that statement.

But, the "new atheists" are apparently completely ignorant of this fact (or maybe they're ignoring it?). Roy Abraham Varghese says it perfectly: "It would be fair to say that the 'new atheism' is nothing less than a regression to the logical positivist philosophy that was renounced by even its most ardent proponents. In fact, the 'new atheists,' it might be said, do not even rise to logical positivism. The positivists were never so naive as to suggest that God could be a scientific hypothesis—they declared the concept of God to be meaningless precisely because it was not a scientific hypothesis."[3]

"But Richard Dawkins and others are scientists, not philosophers."

Right. But scientists *use* philosophy all the time, which is why it's so clear that scientists can make horrible philosophers. They are simply not trained typically in that field of knowledge. As Antony Flew says, as soon as scientists "are engaged in philosophical analysis, neither their authority nor their expertise as scientists is of any relevance."[4]

Even Albert Einstein dismissed Logical Positivism. He says clearly, "I am not a positivist. Positivism states that what cannot be observed does not exist. This conception is scientifically indefensible, for it is impossible to make valid affirmations of what people 'can' or 'cannot' observe. One would have to say 'only what we observe exists,' which is obviously false."[5]

"Huh."

Now you see how the new atheism argues? First, you claim that God is a creature in space. Second, you claim that science gives us all knowable knowledge. Third, you claim that science can't demonstrate God. Therefore, you conclude that God doesn't exist. Richard Dawkins and others demonstrate this reasoning on a regular basis in books and debates. Unfortunately, as you can see, Logical Positivism, or scientism, still has a lingering strength in our culture in spite of the fact that no serious philosopher holds to it.

Ian H. Hutchinson, Professor of Nuclear Science and Engineering at MIT, critiques scientism perfectly:

"Surely if ever there were a topic that is not a question of science, it is metaphysics, theology, and the existence of God. The only way that Richard Dawkins' assertion could possibly make some kind of intellectual sense is in the context of scientism. . . . Under scientism, God is a 'scientific hypothesis like *any* other.' But scientism is a fallacy. . . [I]nsisting that God's existence is a *scientific* question is a giant leap further that only the most blatant scientism could justify. That today's atheists can get away with this scientistic presumption without being summarily dismissed is a sign of how rampant scientism is in our culture today."[6]

He's right. This view is still lingering in our society even though it's been dismissed in scholarly circles for sixty years. So many scientists today—even leading ones!—still think that science is the chief, if not only, real way of knowing something.

Stephen Hawking says this explicitly in his recent book, *The Grand Design*: "Traditionally [questions such as 'What is reality?' or 'Did the universe need a Creator?'] are questions for philosophy, but philosophy is dead. Philosophy has not kept up with modern developments in science, particularly physics. Scientists have become the bearers of the torch of discovery in our quest for knowledge."[7] What an arrogant (or utterly ignorant) and incoherent thing to say. It's mere ignorance or arrogance to believe that scientists are the only persons who give us knowledge.

"Perhaps he meant *scientific* knowledge."

Perhaps. But that's not what he said. Moreover, you don't claim that "philosophy is dead" and then write an entire book on the philosophy of science.[8] This is incoherent. The Oxford scientist and mathematician John Lennox does an excellent job reviewing Hawking's book in *Stephen Hawking and God*. Again, brilliant scientists *can* make embarrassing philosophers.

So Hawking, and anyone else who believes in Logical Positivism or scientism, has eradicated psychology, law, economics, sociology, music, art, ethics, and theology: crucial fields that humans have explored for millennia. For Hawking, why is it OK to dismiss these fields? They are all "dead" fields. Why? Because only scientists discover knowledge. Why? Because only matter and energy exist and scientists study matter and energy.

This is simply false. Are you ready to abandon all these fields just so you can say that science is the only form of real knowledge?

"OK. But religion gets us nowhere. If it were up to the ancient Hebrews, we'd still believe the Earth had four corners. The universe is phenomenally more complex than that. And science is the way we know anything that's true."

You don't really believe that.

"Of course I do. The Earth is not flat."

Of course. Wait . . . it's not? [Laughs] You're right; they were wrong about that, along with every other ancient person. And if the Bible was a twenty-first century science textbook, it should be quickly dismissed.

I was talking about the last thing you said. I don't think you realize what you're saying. If you did, you'd probably be embarrassed.

"What?"

Are you telling me that all truth is known through the scientific method? You know, making a hypothesis, testing the hypothesis, etc.?

"Exactly."

Are you sure? You're telling me that nothing is true unless science proves it?

"Yes. David, I think you're having a hard time with this concept."

Do you believe that last statement was *true*?

"Yes."

Prove it scientifically.

"I can't. It's assumed to be true because . . . Oh."

This is why I said you'd probably be embarrassed. You were making a self-refuting statement. The statements, "the universe is all there is," and "science proves everything," *cannot be proven scientifically.* "That's one of the long-recognized philosophical insufficiencies of the scientistic viewpoint: scientific knowledge itself rests upon lots of non-scientific and unspecifiable 'personal knowledge' possessed by humans. Scientism cannot account for science itself."[9] That is, they are statements that, if true, are beyond scientific evidence. This is why scientism is a fallacy: it's self-refuting.

"And this is why you had the analogy of your brother?"

Yes. If you come to the table ruling out the existence of God, *it's because you hold to a particular worldview*, materialism or naturalism, which disallows anything *outside of* the universe to exist. It's like saying, "In the way that I understand reality, brothers do not exist. Now prove he does exist. And, you can only use the scientific method to prove it." If you already *disbelieved* in the existence of brothers, then nothing I can ever say will convince you otherwise.

And this is crucial to understand: the evidence of my brother had *nothing to do with whether or not you were convinced; your predetermined worldview already had you convinced.* This is why the chief question is: do you have a worldview that makes sense? Or, to put it another way, is your worldview true?

This is why I have no problem saying that leprechauns or unicorns could exist: I do not hold to a worldview that precludes their existence. There is nothing in the way that I see or understand the universe that makes their existence impossible or very, very unlikely.

If you're a materialist, fine. It just means you believe in something that is self-refuting: the *belief* that all that exists is matter and energy is not made of matter or energy. Beliefs are not made of matter or energy. And I could never believe in something that is so patently self-refuting. On top of all this, there are numerous things that every-one knows are true facts but they are not made of matter or energy, nor can they be proven by the scientific method.

"Like what?"

I can think of several[10]: (1) The laws of mathematics. Science can never tell me how or why 2 + 2 = 4, yet everyone knows it's true. So, science cannot prove them and these laws have no physical proper-ties whatsoever.

(2) The laws of logic. People—scientists, historians, medical pro-fessionals—rely upon logic every single day to make decisions. The laws of logic are beyond the realms of science and these laws have no physical properties whatsoever.

(3) Metaphysical truths. Science can tell me all kinds of things about how the brain works and what chemicals are produced when I feel in love, but the questions, "What is a mind?" or "What is justice?" could never be answered by science.

We just assume that other minds exist and that their minds are distinct from our own. Minds are not like laws; they are entities or beings. And our minds have the capacity to reason. Reason cannot be just random biochemical reactions in our brain, or we would have no reason to trust that our thoughts are true. If our thoughts are just the movements of atoms, it means our thoughts are not authorita-tive. This means that *the thought I just had concerning the movement of atoms can't be trusted either*. This kind of reductionism—that is, we are *nothing but* atoms in motion driven by non-rational pro-cesses—is self-refuting because it means the statement we just had about being atoms in motion shouldn't be trusted to be true.

Moreover, we just assume that all kinds of convictions are true, like having trust in my wife, even though it is beyond scientific proof. We could say a whole lot more about metaphysical truths, but let's keep going.

(4) The laws of morality. Now I know that you'll want to talk more about this later, and I'd love to. My point here is only this: if objective morals do exist (and they do), then they are not proven by scientific

methods, nor do they have physical properties. The belief that "rape is wrong" is clearly beyond the realm of science and it has no physical properties.

(5) Aesthetic values. There is no scientific reason for humans to care so much about beauty. Science has no capacity in telling me whether or not Beethoven was a genius or moron, or whether Shakespeare was a novice or master. We "just know" the difference. Aesthetic values are not made of matter or energy.

(6) The scientific method. And as I've already mentioned, the scientific method itself cannot be proven by science, nor does it have any physical properties. Yet, there isn't a scientist on the planet who doesn't rely upon the scientific method every day.

"Wait a second. David, if you have a stroke or whatever, a person's mind seems to be directly affected. And what about all the mentally-handicapped people?"

Good points. There is no doubt that the grey matter of the brain and the mind are related. They are related just as pen and paper are related to communication. If I lose pen and paper, then written communication is impossible. The brain and the mind are most certainly related, but they are most certainly not the same thing.

And this is very important to remember: Reason is not an instinct or feeling or sensation. C.S. Lewis is correct: Reason "is not an object which knocks against us, nor even a sensation which we feel. Reasoning doesn't 'happen to' us: we *do* it."[11]

Now, if we can't trust our Reason to be outside of the cause-and-effect chain of events in Nature, then we are really sunk. It means we have no free-will to make inferences into reality. This would mean that everything we're thinking is conditioned by a need to survive. If Reason is just "natural," or if our thoughts are just what happens when "the laws of nature do their thing" in our brains, then Reason can't be trusted as "true."

"OK. That makes sense. But . . . I can see why someone would believe in 2+2=4, even though no one can *see* that mathematical truth, but it's a different thing—isn't it?—to believe in a *being* that can't be seen?"

Well, if you believe in scientific and mathematic laws then it means there is a metaphysical realm. If there is a metaphysical realm, then there is no reason why a supernatural being couldn't exist. At this point, I'm mostly concerned about your being open to the fact that matter and energy are not all that exists.

But we can say more than that: I believe your *mind* exists, which *is you.* You are a personality, character, or entity, even though I can't see a mind or personality at all. I'm limited to seeing your skin and hair, and surely you think that you are more than skin and hair! Of course, I don't think you—as a being or entity—exist *just because I can see your skin.* The *real you,* the part of you that wills, reasons, and imagines, and controls your body is unseen. Yet, I have no reason to doubt you exist, nor do I demand scientific evidence of your existence. Now, I'll admit – I'm accustomed to meeting other entities because they have bodies. Creatures on our planet have a "shell." I concede that.

"But you don't think your god has a 'shell'?"

That's right. The God that I believe in is not a Being that is like any creature on this planet, or universe, for that matter. This God has no physical limitations unless God chooses to enter into the universe (which, of course, is what Christians believe happened in Jesus).

And I really hope you get this point: The reason why I *believe that the real You*—your mind or personality, something I would call a "soul"—exists is *because of the affect that you have on controlling your body and in your communication to me (because it demonstrates a mind which causes things).* That is, I can't see your soul; I can only see the affect your soul has on your body. Or to say it as philosophers do, you have "intentional agency." That's how I know that God exists, because of the *affect that He has on me and those who believe in Him.*

So, if a metaphysical being can't exist because I can't see Him or touch Him, then you and I don't exist either. And that's a bummer.

"Why did you call God 'Him'?"

Because I'm a Christian. Jews and Christians don't believe God is a male or has an XY chromosome. Ancient Jews referred to God in masculine terms because it distinguished them from every other ancient culture and religion. They were adamant about this point, which was unlike their ancient neighbors: we are not birthed by God. We didn't come from his spit, urine, or semen—things common in other ancient creation stories. That is, we humans are not made *of* God (as if God were cosmic clay) or birthed by God. God created us. He is Creator and we are creature. This is emphasized by understanding God as "He" instead of "She," since a "She" could give birth to us. Also, referring to God as male evoked images of protection and provision to an ancient Mediterranean person.

"Huh" . . . [ponders for a bit] . . . "If materialism is false because there are so many examples of things that are not made of matter or energy, nor can they be proved by science, which means scientism is false, then why do so many atheist scientists and historians and . . . well, every intelligent person I know, believe in Materialism?"

[Laughing] Well, I'd like to think I'm a little intelligent, too. But perhaps I'm not . . .

"I didn't mean . . ."

Of course not. In my experience, I've never met an atheist that wasn't an atheist because of emotional, psychological, or moral reasons. I really don't mean this disrespectfully, but anyone who is adamant about being an atheist is either confused or intellectually dishonest. There is simply no way that one can reasonably say, "I am absolutely convinced that there is no God," because there is no conclusive proof that God doesn't exist. In other words, there is no proof for atheism.

"Wait a second. No one can prove a negative assertion. The burden of proof falls on you."

That's simply not true. You can provide evidence for a negative. William Lane Craig was once told by an Australian forensic scientist: "'Absence of evidence is not evidence of absence.' A suspect might still be the murderer even if there is no evidence that he is. To rule him out, you need an alibi, that is, positive evidence that he did not commit the crime. To rule out God's existence, the atheist needs more than just absence of evidence; he needs some positive evidence of absence."[12]

I can prove that Santa Claus doesn't exist because we can actually go to the North Pole. I can prove that you didn't murder that person on Monday night because I can have video of you across town at the time the person was murdered. I can prove that I didn't take your watch because I can demonstrate that it's still on your wrist. Therefore, it is certainly possible to prove, or at least make a compelling argument for, the negative. So, if a person says, "there is no god," then that person must present some evidence of that belief. Just as if a person says, "I did not murder that person" or "there is no such thing as Santa Claus," evidence must be given.

This is why modern atheists have changed the definition of atheism from "God does not exist" to be "I don't *believe* god exists." This is just an admission of ignorance. This doesn't make one an atheist, it makes one an agnostic: a person who is *uncertain* if God exists. The best a person can say is, "I don't know because I don't find the evidence compelling." That's fair enough. I come to a different conclusion, but I respect that position.

"But those 'negatives' you could demonstrate are material—Santa, a video, and a watch. How can I disprove God's existence if God isn't material?"

Well, there *isn't* any material evidence that God doesn't exist. At best, one could argue that we should expect *more evidence* than what we have, but to do so is pure speculation. If we make it through all the reasons why I believe in God, I think you'll see that there are *more than enough* reasons to believe.

But this just proves my point: it makes no sense to say that one is *certain* that God doesn't exist if you cannot demonstrate evidence that you are correct. To be certain of a negative, you need some evidence to prove it.

"But you're an atheist too. You don't believe in a whole host of gods, like you said. I'm just not certain that one more of those gods exist."

You're right. We are only one god removed from each other. What difference does this make?

"I'm just saying that we're not that different. And . . . just like you don't believe in Zeus, I don't believe in your god."

We're not that different because of that one god?

"Right."

Are you married?

"No."

So, you are just one woman away from being married. You really think that a married person and a bachelor are basically the same or not that far removed?

In any case, you're right that one god isn't *many* gods removed from you—just one. Yet, like I've said, the one God in whom I believe has given us reasons to believe in Him. I can find no such reasons for other gods.

[Pause]

In any case, back to your question, I can think of a few reasons why someone would reject the belief in God or Christianity.

(1) One of the most common reasons I've encountered as a reason for atheism is the belief that believing in religion is for idiots . . . morons . . . for the intellectually enslaved. These kinds of atheists are

convinced that believing in God will make them, or demonstrate that they are, brainwashed, or worse, stupid. The peer pressure in this regard is overwhelming. In order to feel valuable among your other "smart" friends, you simply *must* not believe in God. "Be free of the chains of faith! Come forth and be set free!" And the crowd cheers.

Now, I've met some stupid Christians. I've also met stupid atheists. I'm uncertain what this demonstrates. In any case, the history of science, music, art, mathematics, history, education, and theology make it abundantly clear that "religious" does *not* equal "stupid" or "uninformed." C.S. Lewis says it well: "We know, in fact, that believers are not cut off from unbelievers by any portentous inferiority of intelligence or any perverse refusal to think. Many of them have been people of powerful minds."[13] I wonder how such influential Christians such as G.K. Chesterton or John Milton, Augustine or Thomas Aquinas, Rembrandt, Bach or Handel, Newton or Kepler, would think about this widespread belief among atheists that the true *intelligentsia*, the real erudite, the true scholars, are all materialists. This is mere nonsense. Nevertheless, there are atheists all over the world right now who refuse to believe in God because they are desperately afraid of being considered "backwoods" or "duped" or "stupid" or "crazy" by their peers. Peter Atkins goes so far as to suggest that persons who have abandoned their atheism for belief in God are all experiencing the early onset of senility.[14] Does such a ridiculous claim even need a response?

Brilliant scientists and philosophers are abandoning atheism all the time. A list of *former* atheists would have to include the scientist and theologian Alister McGrath of Oxford; the esteemed geneticist Francis Collins, whom I've already mentioned; C.S. Lewis, the great critic of medieval and Renaissance literature at Oxford; and the philosopher of Yale and Boston University, J.N. Findlay. Antony Flew, the most well-known atheist philosopher of the previous century, left atheism and confessed a belief in an intelligent Creator God.

Again, you have to keep up the rhetoric in your mind to be an active atheist: "Religious people are all stupid and enslaved. I want to be free, so I must fight the urge. Stay free. Don't be like the masses. You're too smart for that. Don't forget—you're smarter than they are. You've figured something out that they just can't see. Stay firm. Feels good, right? You're part of an elite crowd now. You're in a crowd of about 5% of people on the planet. It feels good to be better than them all. All of those 6+ billion people on the planet are so stupid to believe in a Higher Power. You're too smart. Stay strong. There is no god; there is no god; there is no god."

(2) Another reason atheists give for their atheism is that they were really hurt by people who claimed to be religious. I have profound empathy for people who have been hurt by "religious" people. John Loftus, who once claimed to be a Christian, left the faith because of the emotional pain he experienced (along with various unanswered questions he had). He is explicit: *"These are the three things that changed my thinking: a major crisis, plus new information that caused me to see things differently, minus the sense of a loving, caring, Christian community."*[15]

"I guess you've never been hurt by your perfect Christian friends."

I absolutely have! The most intense pain I've ever felt has come from the pain caused by Christians. Betrayal and evil actions are possible even from those who claim to be redeemed by Jesus. For many atheists I've met, they refuse to be open to God's existence because it would involve, in their minds, opening wounds from which they are still healing. However, the healthy response to trauma is grief, not rejecting your faith.

I fully understand the thought, "I'll never believe in a religion that produces that kind of person." Yet, the truth claims of any religion stand or fall *on the founder* of the faith—Moses, Jesus, Mohammed, Mahavira, Kung fu tze, etc.—not on the adherents. Even if every single scientist who followed Einstein were hateful, vengeful punks, it wouldn't mean for one second that we would be compelled to reject $E=mc^2$. That is, general relativity would *not be considered false if those who agreed with Einstein were hypocritical punks*. Of course, if a person had very negative experiences with scientists, then that person would probably not pursue a life of science. In the same way, you might not *want* to be a Christian because of horrible Christians, but it wouldn't mean that the *truth claims of Christianity* are false.

Nevertheless, I really do understand that the greatest problem with Christianity is Christians. I shudder at the thought of how many people *I've* unintentionally turned away from Christianity. We are the number one reason why people are turned off by Christianity, even though we can also be the number one reason people consider it.

(3) Another common reason for being an atheist is that religion is seen as so primitive. That is, to believe in religion is to be backwards, regression, passé. Humans are about progress, they believe, and religion reminds us of our ignorance about the world. This view is especially common among new atheists.

(4) Perhaps, and this has been studied by at least one psychologist, there was a break down in the atheist's relationship with his/her father.[16] It is staggering how frequent it is that well-known atheists have delinquent or evil fathers.

(5) Perhaps atheists don't want to believe in someone that tells them what to do. As Christopher Hitchens was known for saying often in debates, he'd never believe in a "divine dictator" or "divine tyrant" or, my favorite, a "celestial North Korea."

It's a whole lot easier living a life with no moral consequences if you can ignore a Moral Law Giver. I once worked with a woman who said she could never believe in Christianity because, as she said: "I could never believe in a religion that says I can't have sex unless I'm married." That's all it takes. No arguments; no evidence. Just sex. Tell me I can't have it, and I'll never follow that religion.

(6) Perhaps you've been an atheist for so long, or family or friends with other atheists for so long, that you just don't want to change. Believing in God or Christianity might mean you'd have to lose close family or friends who wouldn't understand why you're not the same anymore. I once had an atheist student tell me after hearing most of the evidence I'll give you in our conversation—if you want to stay that long!—that he understood it all and thought it was compelling. He then concluded, "But . . . that's a big decision. So much would have to change in my life." I concurred. It is a big decision. In any case, that's all it takes for him: he didn't want to change his lifestyle.

(7) Or, perhaps, atheists simply don't like the idea. Maybe rigorous

autonomy, you know, just wanting to live on your own, is appealing.

As physicist and cosmologist, Paul Davies says, "There is no need to invoke anything supernatural in the origins of the universe or of life. I have *never liked* the idea of divine tinkering: for me it is much more inspiring to believe that a set of mathematical laws can be so clever as to bring all these things into being."[17]

Beside fatal flaws in his understanding of science, which I can talk about later if you want, his quote demonstrates that he *just doesn't like* any divine causation. One wonders why divine causation is so repulsive to him.

I guess most of these reasons have one thing in common: self-deception. J. Budziszewski, Professor at the University Texas at Austin received his PhD from Yale University. He abandoned all of his childhood belief in Christianity and God throughout all his formal education. He rejected not only God, but any form of objective morality.[18] However, he eventually abandoned his rigorous atheism for Christianity. He believes that "at the bottom of all atheism is self-deception," and by that he means, "pretending to ourselves that we don't know what we really do; it means playing at being ignorant though we are really in the know."[19]

"Yeah, but, I know plenty of people who would feel so helpless and hopeless if they didn't believe in God. Certainly people believe in Christianity because they want to believe in some loving, Santa Claus in the sky."

Now that would be cool! Santa Claus-on-High. This would radically change the way we write Christmas songs. Of course, unlike the belief in God, I've never heard, read, or met anyone in the world who has come to believe in Santa Claus *later* in life.[20] Yet, adult atheists are converting every day.

On your second point, I agree. There certainly are people who believe in Christianity, or God, because they *want* it to be true. Yet, I agree with C.S. Lewis when he says that "the assumption that every man would be pleased, and nothing but pleased, if only he could conclude that Christianity is true, appears to me to be simply preposterous."[21] The demands of Christianity are anything but hedonistic. That is, Christianity is most certainly *not* a religion of getting whatever you want when you want it.

But surely this is irrelevant. A person may be a Christian because that person wants it to be true; an atheist may be an atheist because that person wants it to be true. "Surely these possibilities cancel one another out?"[22]

My point was *not* to demonstrate that Christians are dispassionate and have no psychological motivation, while atheists are merely driven by their feelings. Rather, it was to answer your question: If materialism is self-refuting and has so many counter-examples, why do so many people believe it? I'm just suggesting that there seem to be numerous psychological and moral reasons for believing in atheism. This doesn't mean atheism is false. It just means that we all have our motives. No human is Vulcan (do you know Star Trek?): driven only by the canons of logic or scientific evidence. At the same time, while motives might matter in the discussion, motives don't make facts true or false. This is why I don't spend much time talking about motives, though I talked about it now because you asked me what I thought. I'm much more interested in the reasons people have for their beliefs.

"So if we all have motives, how do we decide which one is right? If there are so many opinions, who's to say? Everyone thinks she or he is right."

We decide what's true by examining the *reasons* one gives for his or her belief, without a predetermined belief about where the reasons will lead us.

"So you're telling me it's all about worldview. I think I understand that point. But why should I believe in your worldview? What makes yours true?"

Well, there are several reasons why my worldview is true. It comes down to a few things (1) materialism is clearly false; (2) another worldview must be true, one which allows for something *other than the universe to exist*; (3) there are scientific facts that strongly suggest a Creator God; (4) there are historical facts that demonstrate that Christianity is true; and (5) I've had religious experience which confirms it all. You could call this worldview, "supernaturalism."

"So, you're saying that a person's worldview is the starting point when thinking about God?

Yes. And I've ranted so much about materialism because every atheist I've ever met holds this worldview. Like I've said, there's only one problem with it: it turns out to be self-refuting and nonsensical. This is no small point: *matter and energy cannot be all there is because we have facts and entities that are not made of matter or energy.* The universe does exist; it's just not the *only* thing that exists. This leads us to the unavoidable conclusion that it is conceivably *possible* that a supernatural being *might* exist. It doesn't mean that God *does exist*; it just means there is no reason to rule God's existence before we've begun. *There is nothing guarding against it.*

I also argued that scientism or Logical Positivism is false: *science cannot prove all things, nor is it the only source of knowledge.* This leads us to the conclusion that there are truths about reality which science cannot possibly prove, but we know for a fact to be true. There are a whole host of things that we know to be true based on our interior perception, but have no scientific data. This will be important to remember when we discuss God's existence.

CHAPTER THREE

Scientific evidence for God and the meaning of "belief"

"This seems so complex. See, if God were real, all she'd have to do is make it clear. It would be so easy to make me believe."

There's a lot you just said that I won't tackle right now, like the fact that I don't believe God should be understood as a "she." But besides that point, I don't find it *too* complex. Besides, I'm not sure what complexity has to do with it. Were you as incredulous when you learned of protons and electrons in the composition of an atom? Do you demand the same simplicity in chemistry, physics, or engineering? My point is that everything in reality is complex when you *really* know something about it. A chair is "simple" to the layperson; to the chemist it's a combination of billions and billions of highly complex atoms held together by various intricate forces.

If you were to ask me how I know I'm in a love relationship with my wife (something which has no scientific data), I couldn't explain it in one sentence. For example, if I said, "I just know we're in love," you'd probably say, "Well, that's nice for you. But I'm not convinced at all. You could be delusional. I've never met her. You could have made up this love relationship because you saw your parents in love. Or, you could say . . . or you could say . . ." and the theories would come pouring out.

If you were open-minded to my being in love with my wife, my evidence would involve all sorts of things: historical stories of when we met, descriptions of her words and behavior toward me, and my interior feelings that corroborate how I feel toward her, amongst other things. All of these things would point to the fact that we have a love relationship, but none of it would absolutely prove it. While there is scientific proof that my wife exists (ignoring the philosophical questions of what existence is!), there is no scientific proof that my wife and I are in a love relationship. Again, there is no scientific proof for certain things because of the *nature* of the thing being argued. That's all I'm arguing right now: some things can't be proven by science, but we *know* they're true.

Second, I've heard this charge a lot: "It'd be so easy for me to believe." Or, "Why wouldn't God make it obvious for everyone?" I don't mean this disrespectfully, but I don't believe you. Everyone *does* have access to God. All of creation cries out the planning of a Creator. As an ancient Hebrew poet said about three thousand years ago: "The heavens declare the glory of God, and the sky above proclaims his handiwork" (Ps 19:1). A Jewish-Christian theologian named Saul expressed a similar idea about two thousand years ago: "[God's] invisible attributes, namely, his eternal power and divine nature, have been clearly perceived, ever since the creation of the world, in the things that have been made" (Rom 1:20). I think they're right. I think the universe's existence demands an explanation given by the existence of God. I'll talk more about this later if you'd like.

In addition, everyone feels the moral compass planted into us by the moral God. Finally, if you honestly looked at all the reasons for why Christianity is true, then I can't fathom why anyone would say, "no."

"I guess I mean that it'd be easier for me to believe in god if I could see god, or if He wrote His name in the sky or parted the Mississippi River or something."

I can certainly relate to the desire to see God. I really can. Yet, if you *need* this to believe in God, this conversation will be very disappointing to you (especially if you were blind!). I believe in a God who, *by definition*, is *not* composed of matter and energy. He is not made of matter or energy no more than a painter is composed of paint or a potter is composed of clay. The painter might get paint *on* herself, but in no way is she *made of* paint.

So, if at the end of our conversation you're still waiting for me to say, "And here is a picture of God, and here is a sample of his blood," then you'll be disappointed. I'm admitting to you as clear as I know how: there is no evidence *like that* that I can give you. "We cannot see God; we cannot touch him; we cannot demand that he give a public demonstration of his existence or character."[1]

Concerning miracles, remember, according to Christianity, God's goal for us is not to see things that make us shriek back in horror or stand in awe, but to participate in a free, loving relationship with Himself. If we saw writing in the sky—let's say it said, "I'm real. Repent and put your trust in me"—two things would certainly happen: (1) Materialists would make excuses for the abnormal cloud formation in the atmosphere that day and say that it is highly more likely that it is a freak movement of air than a miracle; (2) Others might be open to God's existence, be amazed for a while, and eventually go back to their lives.

"But God could appear to everyone."

Oh, He will. But when He does, it won't be time to make up your mind if you believe in Him. Time as we know it will be over and what we really believe about God will be made manifest.

My point is, miracles don't ever illicit proper faith in and love for God. They never have. Ever. The ancient Hebrews apparently had several miracles performed for them and before hardly any time had passed, the shock and awe had rubbed off and they were back to their unfaithful, unloving ways again. We see the exact same thing in Jesus' lifetime. Even after all his miracles, guess how many people stayed faithfully by His side all the way to the cross? No one. Gregory Boyd is right: "Precisely because the event is extraordinary, the mind seems to remember it more like a dream than a real event. It doesn't continue to impact life. If a person does base his faith on miracles, he needs a steady diet. But then the miracles stop being miraculous."[2]

So, I concur: more "sea partings" would be cool to see, but they wouldn't attract us to love God any more at all.

"Then why did they happen?"

They seem to have occurred to confirm divine revelation.

"Hmm. Well, I don't see any reason to believe in miracles anyway, not to mention a god up there. So, if you can't give me scientific evidence for God, then why do so many Christians act like they have scientific proof?"

Well, I can't speak for other Christians. Yet, I do think this is a very common misunderstanding.

The God that Christians believe in is not a creature in this universe. Rather, He is a Triune, transcendent, all-powerful, all-knowing, timeless, immaterial, personal, loving, and moral being. That is the God we believe in. Of course there is no scientific evidence for God: science is too small. Francis Collins is correct: "If God exists, then He must be outside of the natural world, and therefore the tools of science are not the right ones to learn about Him."[3] Finally, Christians believe that this God revealed Himself inside the universe through Jesus of Nazareth.

"I do remember reading Richard Dawkins: 'the presence or absence of a creative super-intelligence is unequivocally a scientific question.'"[4]

I really understand what Dawkins is doing. The only way to defeat Theism is by completely redefining what we mean by a "creative super-intelligence." Unfortunately, Dawkins is just completely wrong. No Theist believes that a "creative super-intelligence" is a creature *within* the universe.

Instead, Alister McGrath's comments are right on: "Scientific atheists challenge Christians to prove the existence of God, as if Christians understand God to be an object within the world—such as an additional moon orbiting the planet Mars, a new species of newt or an invisible unicorn. Perhaps they think Christians imagine God to be like an Olympian deity, sitting on the top of Mount Olympus, waiting patiently to be discovered."[5]

This reminds me of what Nikita Khrushchev, former leader of the Soviet Union, said concerning Yuri Gargarin's monumental arrival in space in 1961: "Gagarin flew into space, but didn't see any god there."[6] [Laughing] If you listened closely, you could have heard monotheists all over the world say simultaneously, "of course not."

McGrath continues: "One of the more puzzling features of Dawkins's new atheism is his apparently unquestioned assumption that the theist's inventory of the universe simply includes one extra (and totally unnecessary) item that is absent from an atheists' list. The universal inventory must be open to verification by scientific methods. And as the existence of this God cannot be scientifically proved, it is to be dismissed as having vanishingly small probability. Dawkins does not believe in such a God. But then, neither do I."[7]

So to reiterate: I can produce no scientific proof for God's existence. As the German theologian Dietrich Bonheoffer said, "A god who let us prove his existence would be an idol."[8] Rather, I believe that certain scientific truths can be used *to infer the existence of God*. Like in so many places (such as law and forensic sciences), we *infer to the best explanation*. This, added with solid historical facts and genuine religious experience, and I'm sold.

"I don't know. I think I need scientific evidence."

If scientific evidence is all that will convince you, then you have no reason to trust philosophical truths, aesthetic values, emotions, virtues, mathematics, or logic, or that anything occurred at all in history. So much of what we cherish and believe to be true in life is not *perceived* with sense, but known through intuition. There are soldiers sacrificing their lives every single day for things they could never possibly see—justice, freedom, and human rights.

But, I need to be very clear at this point: my Christian faith is not in science. I believed in God long before I knew of DNA or the Big Bang. However, there have been atheists who have converted to Christianity because of scientific discovery. Not so for me. I do think certain scientific facts support God's existence, but like I said, my faith is not in the changing discoveries of scientists.

"Then why do Christians seem to believe in God because of what science discovers?"

Unfortunately, I know some Christians base their faith partly or solely in scientific discovery, but this is certainly misplaced and dangerous. It's misplaced because the truth claims of Christianity have never been based on scientific discovery (even though scientific discovery has bolstered the faith of most scientists throughout history). The church did not begin because Aristarchus of Samos produced the first heliocentric model of the universe!

It's dangerous because scientific discovery is constantly changing previously-held views. Francis Collins gives the same warning: "Faith that places God in the gaps of current understanding about the natural world may be headed for crisis if advances in science subsequently fill those gaps. Faced with incomplete understanding of the natural world, believers should be cautious about invoking the divine in areas of current mystery, lest they build an unnecessary theological argument that is doomed to later destruction."[9] Fortunately, the central truth claims of Christianity are based on compelling historical evidence, not the shifting sands of science.

"Then how do you sense God if you can't touch him?

I know God exists because of my *interior perception of Him*. Remember the analogy with my wife? I believe that we are in a love relationship—something that cannot be proved scientifically and is not made of matter or energy—because of a feeling I have that is based on a whole host of things, such as how she treats me, how she looks at me, how we live, etc. In a similar way, belief that God exists and trusting in Him is based on a whole host of things, such as certain scientific facts that point to God, historical evidence of Jesus, human moral intuition, and religious experience.

"Then I think I'm confused about what you mean by 'believe.'"

This is a great *point*. I'm glad you mentioned it. We typically say that we "know" something to be true when we have no doubt at all. In most cases, this kind of "knowing" comes from tactile evidence. I would say that I know my kids exist because I have physical and emotional evidence along with corroboration from my wife. That is, I can touch them, I have feelings in response to them, and my family and friends corroborate their existence. I could say that I'm 100% certain that they exist (or maybe 99.999%). Of course, I could be delusional and lied to, but this seems preposterous given the nature and preponderance of the evidence.

"Belief" in modern English is different. We usually say it when we are expressing doubt. "I *believe* the meeting is tonight (but it could be tomorrow)."

When Christians use the word "believe" and "belief," we're *not using it that way*. "Belief" has never, in the history of Christianity, meant a "blind leap of faith" into the unknown. It's more like saying, "I believe you and I are having this conversation right now." The New Testament uses a Greek word that is best understood as a *reasonable* "trust." I trust that you and I are having this conversation because of multiple reasons. Or I could say that I put my trust in my wife because I believe certain things about her. I believe that she exists and that we have a love relationship.

As usual, C.S. Lewis says it perfectly: "Belief, in this sense, seems to me to be assent to a proposition which we think so overwhelmingly probable that there is a psychological exclusion of doubt, though not a logical exclusion of dispute."[10] That is, we believe something that is not 100% certain, but so probable that not believing in it would seem absurd.

It seems that so many people, especially atheist authors today, confuse two very different stages of a person's belief in Christianity: (1) the "way in which a Christian first assents to certain propositions and (2) the way in which he afterwards adheres to them."[11] These are not the same thing and they should be kept distinct in our minds.

Besides a rare few, Christians have always *come to believe in* Christianity because of various evidences, whether logical proofs, scientific discoveries, religious experiences, literary evidence, or on the authority of others. I know this is true for me. There is no seriously-thinking Christian I have ever heard of or met who initially believes in Christianity without any shred of evidence of that belief. "You ought to believe in Jesus." – "Why? Who's that?" – "Don't worry about that, just believe." – "Oh, OK." Who would do this?

The original intellectual assent is predicated upon certain evidential facts.

"But isn't Richard Dawkins correct when he insists that if you do have evidence, then it's no longer faith?"

Yeah; I've heard him say that in multiple interviews and debates. At a speech delivered to the American Humanist Association in 1996, Richard Dawkins said, "Science is based upon verifiable evidence. Religious faith not only lacks evidence, its independence from evidence is its pride and joy, shouted from the rooftops. Why else would Christians wax critical of doubting Thomas?"[12] This demonstrates an ignorance of what Christians actually believe and a misunderstanding of what was going on with Thomas and Jesus in John 20:24-29. One would hope that an opponent of a view would actually know the basic facts of what it is he is attempting to refute.

If he couldn't get past the *assumption* that "faith" or "belief" must mean a blind leap of faith based on no evidence whatsoever, then we would have nothing more to talk about. All I can say is that *his* definition and *Christianity's* definition are utterly different. I can think of a few representative examples. David Wood says, "When I say that I have faith in God, I mean that I place my trust in God based on what I know about him."[13] Or, we could use Alister McGrath's definition: "Faith is not belief without proof but trust without reservetions—trust in a God who has shown himself worthy of that trust."[14] Or, C.S. Lewis' definition might help: "Faith . . . is the art of holding on to things your reason has once accepted, in spite of your changing moods."[15] Do any of these proper definitions of "faith" sound like blind faith?

This would also mean that Dawkins is attempting to refute a religious view *that no one is, in fact, holding to be true.* He's dismantling a strawman, or caricature, of what Christianity is. That should be easy enough to do.

"You mentioned authority as a source of knowledge. So you'd believe in

God just because you trusted someone who told you that?"

I wouldn't, but there are people who do. Yet, this shouldn't be that difficult to allow. Nearly all of our scientific beliefs, "all of our historical beliefs, most of our geographical beliefs, many of our beliefs about matters that concern us in daily life, are accepted on the authority of other human being, whether we are Christians, Atheists, Scientists, or Men-in-the-Street."[16] Of course, for most people, Wikipedia, Twitter, and Facebook are authoritative enough to believe in something.

And I *don't* think understanding "belief" in this sense, that is, being overwhelmingly convinced, but not 100% certain, is reserved for theological issues alone. There are *numerous* things in life about which we have belief, even though there is uncertainty. "The scientific beliefs of those who are not themselves scientists often have this character, especially among the uneducated. Most of our beliefs about other people are of the same sort. The scientist himself . . . has beliefs about his wife and friends which he holds, not indeed without evidence, but with more certitude than the evidence, if weighed in the laboratory manner, would justify."[17]

That is, people believe things with a *high degree* of certainty every single day, even though such belief far exceeds the evidence. People jump into taxies all the time, certain that the drivers are trustworthy and know where they're going. We could list copious examples of such certainty, even though we have no scientific evidence that we should trust the facts or the people as much as the evidence suggests. In fact, we have faith beyond the evidence concerning most things in life.

"You know, this reminds me of another quote from Richard Dawkins that I read: 'Faith, being *belief that isn't based on evidence*, is the principal vice of any religion.'[18]"

It all depends on what Dawkins means by "evidence." Since I think he believes in scientism, I think he means "*scientifically verifiable* evidence." If that's what he means, all I could say is, "Of course not; I don't believe in a god who is made of matter or energy."

Again, if Dawkins thinks that every belief he has in reality is based solely on scientific evidence, then I'd ask Dawkins a question. "Richard, do you *believe* your wife can be trusted around other men? Do you *have faith* in her? If so, what scientific proof do you have?" After stammering around for some time about how "the love of a wife is different," I would respond, "So you must also believe that faith, being belief that isn't based on evidence, is the principal vice of any *relationship*."

To be clear: it is too naïve and simplistic to say that "all I need is evidence to believe in God." It depends on the kind of evidence you're asking for. And since God is not a creature in the universe, we shouldn't expect direct, scientific evidence to be offered for His existence.

Instead, if He is the Creator, *we should expect things He has created to give us clues as to His existence and His character;* much like an architect's existence and character is hinted at in the building she designs.

"Is this the critique of scientism or Logical Positivism you were making earlier?"

That's right. We all know—even scientists!—that scientific knowledge is *not* the chief or only reason why we believe something. In fact, scientists do *not* use the scientific method to discover almost *every bit of knowledge they have.*

I love how C.S. Lewis describes it. He explains how specialists use different methods to determine facts. Mathematicians and scientists use different methods to arrive at knowledge. "Those of the historian and the judge are different again. The mathematician's proof (at least so we laymen suppose) is by reasoning, the scientist's by experiment, the historian's by documents, the judge's by concurring sworn testimony. But . . . on questions *outside their own disciplines,* [they] have *numerous beliefs* to which they do not normally apply the methods of their own disciplines. It would indeed carry some suspicion of morbidity and even of insanity if they did."[19]

"I'm not certain I understand the distinction. This kinda' sounds like slick word games. Isn't belief just belief?"

I don't think so. The process I first took to meet, know, understand, and love my wife is a very different process than the process that *sustains* my love relationship with her.

Being a Christian involves these two steps: first, the initial "courtship"; second, the sustained relationship, even when there seems to be contrary evidence. As C.S. Lewis says, Christians "even warn one another that such apparent contrary evidence—such 'trials of faith' or 'temptations to doubt'—may be expected to occur, and determine in advance to resist them. And this is certainly shockingly unlike the behavior we all demand of the scientist or the historian in their own disciplines."[20]

"Right. If scientists disregarded all forms of doubts in their theories, no one would take them seriously. They wouldn't be serious scientists. Even Francis Collins admits that 'science is progressive and self-correcting: no significantly erroneous conclusions or false hypotheses can be sustained for long, as newer observations will ultimately knock down incorrect constructs.'"[21]

But what if a scientist were faced with the issue of doubting her husband's fidelity? If this doubt occurred, would she just conduct a series of experiments to test that hypothesis with pure neutral motivations?[22] Of course not. The point being, no one is governed by scientific evidence in all areas of life.

What I'm talking about is relational *trust*. Don't forget, Christians believe that God is personal: we can actually have an active relationship with Him. Whenever we are in a relationship with another person, once we accept the other person is real and can be trusted, we must "have faith" on a regular basis, even when there is no evidence to do so, or even when there is counter evidence to do so. We don't praise our friends when they doubt us; we condemn them.[23]

"And you think this is similar to believing in God?"

Yes; the same is true with Christian faith.

"You mean you never question God once you believe? Ever?"

[Laughing] Oh no! Sure I do. In fact, as a Christian, I believe that God wants us to: God likes demonstrating that He can be trusted (cf. Malachi 3:11). Of course, ultimately, we surrender to what He wants because He's the Creator and we're not, and He's shown Himself to be trustworthy. We can trust that what occurs in life is *ultimately* for His good and our good.

Of course, demanding constant evidence from a trusted friend would be strikingly unfair and would damage our relationship.[24] It would demonstrate that our friendship was a farce.

"That's true."

But trust, nevertheless, is exactly what God requires of us once we do believe in Him. And this means there are plenty of times when we don't have evidence that God should be trusted. If God gave you all the evidence you'd ever need, then you'd never trust God any more than you already did. Or think of this way: if I gave my son evidence every single time he doubted me, then he'd never learn *that I can be trusted*. He might see that I can show him proof; He'd learn nothing of my character.

Well, the point I was trying to make through all this is simple: no serious Christian believes in God or Christianity "just because." They have reasons to believe. Then, once we do believe in a particular God, we are asked to trust Him like we might trust a good, loving friend. And it is *this relational trust* that is "shouted from the rooftops": not a blind leap of faith into the unknown.

"I guess I'm still stuck on the idea that something might exist that has no material or chemical properties. But . . . then again, I do believe that I have a mind. I do believe that. I certainly don't think I'm just random chemical reactions."

[Smiles]

"Huh."

CHAPTER FOUR

Scientific facts that point to God: The origin of the universe

"Alright, so why should I believe God exists, even though I can't see 'Him' (as you say)?"

Because once you believe, you receive a cool message-decoder ring and a cape.

[Stares at me.]

I can't *make you* believe anything; just like you can't *make* me believe anything. All I can do is to tell you what *I* find compelling. And for me, there are three different types of evidence that convince me:

(1) I believe that for certain facts God is an Agent cause with the best explanatory power (it best explains the fact being studied) and explanatory scope (it best explains all the details surrounding the fact); (2) there is historical evidence for Christianity (which would mean God does exist); and (3) there is personal experience that conforms to the belief in a particular God. All three involve different types of evidence, none of which could be tested in a laboratory.

Also I need to make clear that I don't believe for just one reason; it's the cumulative case that convinces me. For me, evidence for God is based on a cumulative case.

If He is the Creator, we should expect things He has created to give us clues, that is, to point toward His existence and character. This means that we have evidence, or clues, and then work backwards. This is exactly what forensic specialists do on a daily basis. They see clues and work backward to the cause with the most explanatory power and scope. This is called abductive reasoning.

Moreover, when forensic specialists make their case for a cause, they do not ever "prove" it beyond any doubt. No one in forensic studies needs something to be "proved" with that kind of certainty. They only need it to be beyond reasonable doubt.

"So you admit they don't prove God exists?"

Of course I do! Outside of geometrical proofs, nothing in life is 100% certain or provable. I'm not 100% certain that you exist or that I exist. Yet, and this is very important to understand, I have *sufficient reason* to believe that you and I exist. And that's enough. I don't have 100% certainty that my wife loves me, but I have sufficient reason to believe it. You and I live every single day with uncertainty. The same is true with God's existence.

"But, it's God. Shouldn't we need 100%?"

I do think there are *very compelling reasons to believe* in God. If you need 100%, then you'll be disappointed by my answers.

"OK. Fair enough."

First of all, it should be said that there have been people throughout history who have argued that God's existence doesn't need to be argued at all.

"Huh?"

They would argue that God's existence is foundational, or basic knowledge or brute fact. If I said, "All men are mortal; I am a man; therefore, I am mortal," would this conclusion be true?

"Sure. That's called deductive logic."

Great. How do you know it's true?

[Long pause.]

"I just do. It's just true."

So, there's no scientific or historical evidence for deductive logic?

"Right."

In the same way, there have been many that have argued that God's existence is true in the exact same way. It's *just true*. It's a brute fact.

"Is that what you believe?"

Yes, but I still need some type of evidence. I'm more skeptical . . . especially since we're talking about a Being, not a logical process. Nevertheless, I do partly agree with that understanding of God.

In any case, here's the deal. There are almost an endless amount of questions that humans have about reality. And I don't know of any Christian who thinks that "God" is the answer to every conceivable question. Like I said earlier, we know that the universe is expanding, but no Christian would say that God is pushing the planets away from each other with His divine hands. It might be dark matter and dark energy. Whatever.

Light is made of photons. Why does light travel at the particular speed it does? I don't know why, but I *don't* think God is shoving photons around the universe. Humans will probably discover one day why light travels as fast as it does. The same is true with bees. There is no scientific explanation for why they can fly. But, it'll probably be discovered one day why they can fly.

Scientists aren't certain what gravity is. No Christian would say that God is pushing matter towards other matter with His divine hands. Maybe gravity is a curve in the space-time continuum. Whatever. I could go on and on with examples of things that scientists will one day probably be able to explain.

If Christians were arguing that "God" was the answer to every question then we'd be guilty of the "god-of-the-gaps." That is, whenever there's a question, give God the credit. No serious Christian does that, at least none of whom I'm aware. In any case, *I* don't do that.

However, there are a *few* questions of reality that we have that give me strong reasons to *infer God's existence*. In my opinion, they point to God. That is, God seems to be the best causal explanation for these facts.

Now, I'm not suggesting I'm a Christian because of gaps in our scientific knowledge. Yet, I do think that our scientific knowledge can point to the truth claims of Christianity.

"Are these those things you mentioned when we first started?"

Yes. To make certain we're on the same page, I think the following things point to God: (1) the existence of the universe, (2) the existence of multiple, fine-tuned constants throughout the universe which allow life, (3) the existence of life, (4) the existence of morality, and (5) the existence of the soul. I believe the *nature of these things* suggest God's existence.

And we can't forget: for centuries, every Western scientist assumed God was the answer to why these facts exist (except they didn't know about DNA/RNA) and all questions concerning origins. In fact, it has been argued that the entire Western pursuit of scientific knowledge was predicated on the understanding that the universe was "rational" or comprehensible *because it was designed by God*.

In fact, I could argue that this is the sixth scientific fact that points to God: the intelligibility of nature. The fact that we can discover mathematic formulas that are constant throughout the universe is simply phenomenal. There is no reason at all in atheism to assume that the universe follows any patterns, that there is uniformity. C.S. Lewis says it perfectly: "Men became scientific because they expected Law in Nature, and they expected Law in Nature because they believed in a Legislator. In most modern scientists this belief has died: it will be interesting to see how long their confidence in uniformity survives it."[1] I wonder if Lewis would be surprised sixty years later that atheist scientists still assume laws to be constant across the universe without any conceivable explanation as to why they are.

Ever since the Enlightenment, thinkers have asked the question, "What if we got rid of God as a cause for anything that happens?" Can we still come to credible scientific conclusions if we assume there is no Creator God?

In general, materialist scientists—those who are heirs to the Enlightenment worldview—have exclaimed, "Yes!"

In fact, the answer is certainly, "no," and here's why. The more we learn about the universe, the more order and rationality we discover. There is no scientific explanation whatsoever for the intelligibility of the laws of nature. The only explanation for the *rational* intelligibility of the universe is a divine Mind that gives the universe its laws. It is illogical to argue that the universe could be rationally governed by laws if the universe arose from non-rational, accidental processes. Nevertheless, atheists will continue to trust that the universe is rational, even though it is incoherent to do so in a materialistic worldview.

In fact, the standard mantra of the New Atheists goes further: science and religion simply cannot go together; or worse, science disproves God's existence. We've already discussed how much Richard Dawkins bangs this drum. We could also mention the eminent quantum theorist and cosmologist, Stephen Hawking, who said "There is a fundamental difference between religion, which is based on authority, [and] science, which is based on observation and reason. Science will win because it works."[2]

Such beliefs are clearly against both commonsense and what can be proved by Hawking. The truth claims of Christianity in particular are most certainly not based solely on authority, nor is it void of observation or reason. Moreover, in what way will science "win"? Are they in a race? Does Hawking really think that religious explanations of reality are competing with scientific theories of how matter and energy work? Or perhaps he thinks religious people are studying their holy books to determine how black holes work.

[Pauses]

And I'm uncertain what he means by science winning in the end because "it works." Again, if he means something like, "Theological ideas about God sure make very poor explanations of quantum theory because they sure don't work," then he is quite confused as to the goals and methods of religious inquiry. If he means something even close to such nonsense, then it's difficult to know how to respond.

Must we really be forced into these false alternatives? Must we really choose between science or religion? In the same vein, are we really forced to choose between the culinary arts or chemistry? Mechanical engineering or architecture? Political science or sociology? Of course religion covers aspects of science, but it does so in that science is swallowed up by religion, much like chemistry is swallowed up by culinary arts or engineering is swallowed up by architecture.

"Hmm."

This reminds me of a great quote. Steven Jay Gould, formerly of Harvard University, was considered one of the leading evolutionary biologists of our time. He was a Jewish agnostic. Even he was emphatic on this point: "To say it for all my colleagues and for the umpteenth millionth time: Science simply cannot by its legitimate methods adjudicate the issue of God's possible superintendence of nature. We neither affirm nor deny it, we simply can't comment on it as scientists."[3]

Gould was right. Science and religion are not at war, nor can science prove or disprove God. This is why I get so frustrated when watching T.V., I see a reporter ask a quantum physicist, "So tell me. Does God exist?" This is just like asking the same scientist, "What is the meaning of life?"

Why does the common myth continue to flourish that scientists can answer all questions pertaining to existence? It's because most people believe in scientism: that the scientific method answers every "real" question. As we've already discussed, this is nonsense. Scientists do not have jurisdiction concerning metaphysical truths. It's outside of what they can ever discover. They might be world-class quantum theorists, but they can make horrible philosophers.

However, I do think there are some scientific facts that point to God. I'll explain. Hop in if you have any questions.

(1) Though it took several decades for a consensus to be reached, it is now considered scientific consensus that the universe came into existence around 13.3 to 13.9 billion years ago. (You might know this fact by the name given to it by the scientist Fred Hoyle, the "Big Bang.") This cosmological explanation suggests that all of space, time, matter, and energy in the universe came into being from non-existence. As Stephen Hawking said nearly fifteen years ago, "Almost everyone now believes that the universe and time itself had a beginning at the Big Bang."[4]

Everything that *comes into existence* had a cause, right? Since the universe came into existence, then it must have had a cause. And we can know a few things about this first cause because of the nature of creation. This cause must have been *immaterial* (since matter wasn't created yet), *not made of energy* (since energy wasn't created yet), *timeless* (since time wasn't created yet), *spaceless* (since space wasn't created yet), and very powerful. This is the bare minimum. The cause could *not* be a black hole or some other physical cause because before the Big Bang *nothing* existed. Now, this is solid, deductive reasoning. I've not appealed to the Bible or the Koran or any "holy" book.

Now, the *only two things* that fit this description—that is, are timeless, spaceless, and not made of matter or energy—are *laws* and *minds*.[5]

Yet, scientific, mathematical, logical, and moral laws can't *create* anything. Now, *physical realities* can cause things, such as the sun converting hydrogen into helium plus energy, but the *laws that* describe how physical realities work cannot create. And don't forget: scientific laws aren't like civil laws, such as the law not to break the speed limit. Scientific laws don't tell matter and energy what they can or cannot do. Rather, they just describe what physical realities tend to do in the universe. What about the final kind of law, the Moral Law? The Moral Law only describes the way humans *ought* to behave. So, the Moral Law doesn't create either. Therefore, no law can cause something to come from nothing.

However, minds, or personal agents, are timeless, spaceless, and not made of matter or energy, and they *can* create. Human minds, at least, create ideas nearly every second of consciousness. Therefore, the most rational explanation is that an unimaginably powerful mind created the universe. "That is to say, [what created the universe] is conscious, and has purposes, and prefers one thing to another. And on this view it made the universe, partly for purposes we do not know, but partly, at any rate, in order to produce creatures like itself—I mean, like itself to the extent of having minds."[6]

"That's a far cry from the God of Christianity."

Oh it is! You're right! This doesn't mean that the Trinity exists. The point I'm making now is that it is certainly possible that a powerful mind is Creator. It takes many other things to get to the Trinity. If we have time, I'd like to get to them.

"Well, the cause could be something else."

If there is anything else besides laws and minds that are timeless, spaceless, and not made of matter or energy, then I'm open to hearing them. I've never heard or read of anything else that would fit these properties.

"Still, it could be something else."

[Pauses]

Well, sure, I guess. But this is just a story. If scientists worked this way, then no science would ever occur. We could just say to every single theory ever offered, "It could be something else." Unless you have some evidence of any other abstract object that fits these properties, then you are forced with two, and only two, explanations for a cause of the universe.

"Well, it can't be a mind, or personal agent, because humans can't create matter and energy."

Well, wait a second. I completely concur that *human* agents can't create. But no one argues that. I'm arguing that God, who is not human, yet who is a *personal Agent*, did, in fact, create matter and energy. This is a basic property of a Creator God as offered by every form of monotheism.

"But we have no evidence or example of an unembodied mind. If we have a mind, it's in a human body. Also, we have no evidence of a mind creating matter and energy."

We do have evidence of a mind that is not made of matter or energy—yours and mine. We can talk later about this if you'd like. Also, I agree that we have no example of a mind existing without a body. But what does this prove? It can't possibly prove that a supernatural mind cannot exist.

"But there's no scientific evidence of such a mind. Why believe that a mind can create things or that it can exist apart from a body?"

Asking for scientific evidence of an unembodied mind is like asking for scientific evidence for justice or beauty. These are immaterial facts of existence.

It's true that human minds are associated with bodies but there is no reason to assume *it cannot be otherwise*. In other words, you have no evidence that minds *only and always only* exist in bodies. You might assume that, but that's a false assumption. In order for me to be convinced, I need some reason or argument that minds *cannot* exist without a body.

"If our minds can't create matter and energy, why assume God can?"

Remember, we're talking about what caused the universe to come into being from nothing. A mind is the only option left that is something that is timeless, spaceless, immaterial, not made of energy, and can cause something else. I'm not *assuming* there's a God. I'm saying that we're left with one option *for the universe's* ɔ existence from nothing: a creating mind.

ɔ characteristic, being able to create, has always been a
...ɔɾɪɑl characteristic of what we call, "God." That is, God has
the capacity to do it. I don't. Humans don't. No human can create.
We're not deity. Only deity creates. One way humans are like God is
that *we can cause one type of thing*, that is, ideas, but we are not like
God because we can't cause to bring *material* things into existence.

"I still think believing in a cosmic mind is beyond comprehension."

What's beyond comprehension is the belief that the universe came
from nowhere by nothing. If I had to pick between that option and a
powerful Mind as the Creator, then I'll pick a Creator.

[Long pause.]

"But if there was no time before the universe, then there couldn't be a
cause, since causes must take place in time. In other words, there must
be a sequence."

No, that's not true. It is certainly possible for a cause and its effect
to be coterminous, i.e., to be happening at the same time. I've heard
Dr. William Lane Craig give the analogy of a chandelier hanging from
the ceiling. The cause of the hanging is gravity pulling it down; the
effect is that the chandelier is dangling. The cause and its effect are
happening at the same time. Or, consider a person in a hot tub: while
the person is in the hot tub, the water is displaced. The effect (water
displaced) is happening at the exact same time as the cause (the
person).

"But the question of what was there *before* the universe makes no
sense, since there was no "before" the beginning of time. It's like asking what's north of the North Pole?"

You're right. However, if I asked, "What is the *cause* of the North
Pole?" you certainly wouldn't say, "Nothing . . . it just is . . . because

nothing can be north of the North Pole." Instead, you'd tell me about the Earth's axis of rotation, or if you meant the North Magnetic Pole, you'd talk about an electromagnetic field that causes that polarity.

This is primarily a problem of language. We're talking about the act of creating something from a state of timelessness. If it would help you, I could ask, "What could create time?" or "What is the cause of time?" rather than, "What existed before the universe?"

We have no analogy to this in human comprehension. How could the deep sea lanternfish ever understand what living on dry land and breathing air would be like? I simply can't imagine creating *time itself* or living outside of it, no more than the deep sea fish could imagine walking around on land. The closest that I can think of experiencing some form of timelessness is in my consciousness. My mind doesn't age. I don't "think" older than I used to, even though I feel older.

"If God is eternal, and God created the universe, then why isn't the *universe* eternal? Why did the universe begin thirteen point whatever billion years ago?"

God exists eternally. He can even have *the intention* to create the universe eternally. Yet, as soon as God decided actually *to create* the universe, He made a temporal decision. This would mean that God decided to actually create the universe billions of years ago. William Lane Craig gives a helpful analogy:

"[A] man sitting changelessly from eternity could freely will to stand up; thus a temporal effect arises from an eternally existing agent. Similarly, a finite time ago a Creator endowed with free will could have freely brought the world into being at that moment. In this way, the Creator could exist changelessly and eternally but choose to create the world in time. . . . So the cause is eternal, but the effect is not. In this way, then, it is possible for the temporal universe to have come to exist from an eternal cause: through the free will of a personal Creator."[7]

Now, since time has been created with the universe, God must relate to time in some fashion. Theologians discuss how God relates to or interacts with time, and that's beyond our discussion at this point.

Yet, this is a great time to mention that God is *eternally* creating, one might say. A boat will float for only as long as the laws of buoyancy exist. In the same way, the universe will exist for only as long as God sustains it. God's creative process is ongoing, sustaining and grounding all of our existence. If God were to stop "thinking" of the universe, one might say, then the universe would cease to exist. The universe depends on God to exist; God doesn't need the universe at all.

"But why couldn't the universe have come into existence from nothing?"

[Smiles] Really?

"Yeah, sure, why not?"

Because we have no evidence that anything at all comes into existence from a state of nothingness and there is no evidence to counter this fact. It's safe to say that it is a metaphysical law that *things do not ever come into being without a cause.*

As Greg Koukl said to me once, could you imagine hearing a knock at the door and thinking, "Wow. That was improbable. What are the odds that there was a knock at my door with no cause?" Do knocks knock themselves? What is the first thing we say when we hear a knock at the door?—"Who's there?" I think the universe was "knocked" and I want to ask, "Who's there?"

"But that's begging the question: we all know that knocks are caused by people, so of course you'd ask who's there."

Yep, but my point is this: in the same way that I believe knocks don't spontaneously knock themselves, I believe universes do not spontaneously create themselves. For a universe to create itself, it would have to exist in order to create itself. This is nonsense.

"Stephen Hawking disagrees with you. Well, he does agree that the universe was caused, but just not from a 'Who.' The cause was an 'it.' And to be honest, I'll trust his scientific belief over yours. He says: 'As recent advances in cosmology suggest, the laws of gravity and quantum theory allow universes to appear spontaneously from nothing. Spontaneous creation is the reason there is something rather than nothing, why the universe exists, why we exist.'"[8]

This reminds me of the quote I gave you earlier by Paul Davies, which said he much preferred the idea that "the laws can be so clever as to bring all these things into being."

Any amateur scientist can note quickly how this makes no sense: "mathematical laws" have never, nor could they ever, bring one single thing "into being."[9] Laws describe; they do not create. Moreover, mathematical laws are not "clever"; they are non-rational facts of the universe.

Here is Hawking, making the exact same error: *laws do not and cannot ever create anything.* We've covered this already. Laws are descriptions of the way things are; they are not creative energies. Therefore, the "laws of gravity" or the laws of anything else can't *cause* anything to come into being. Laws might "allow them to appear" (as Hawking said), much like gravity "allows waterfalls to appear" when water goes over a cliff, but laws cannot create. No one would say that the water or the cliff is created out of nothing by gravity or the laws of gravity.

Also, Hawking's use of "nothing" is completely misleading. Doesn't nothing mean "no thing"? How are "laws of gravity" and "gravity" nothing? Where did the laws of gravity come from? Even if we allow for the unverified belief in quantum fluctuations in a vacuum at the Big Bang, where did the vacuum of quantum fluctuations come from? A vacuum is a fluctuation of energy. A quantum vacuum has physical properties: Hawking knows this very well! In other words, Hawking has not told us what caused the *universe* because gravity and quantum fluctuations are *part of the universe.* He hasn't gone back far enough.

It's as if someone were to ask me where my son came from and I said, "a zygote." That doesn't answer the question at all. The zygote is just the first stage of development of my son. A zygote didn't exist eternally in his mother's womb. To understand my son's origin, I have to talk about beings that caused him to come into existence. See my point? Saying the origin of the universe is a quantum vacuum is like saying that my son's origin is a zygote. The question of origins would still be left unanswered.

Since matter and energy, or the laws that govern them, cannot create something from nothing, nor is it possible for something to come into existence without any cause, I'm left with two alternatives: (1) we have no idea how the universe began, and never will know, since the answer is beyond what humans can discover, or (2) an unimaginably powerful mind that transcends the universe brought the universe into existence.

Now, here's the deal: if I had nothing at all to go by—if religion didn't exist and no one had ever thought about a supernatural being, I might stop there. I might just say, like in option one, "Huh . . . it's the greatest mystery we'll ever have and science simply cannot answer the question because science can't know anything beyond the universe." And really, this is exactly what I do say in some sense, because science, though helpful, is very limited as to what it can help us know. Yet, since matter and energy are not all that exists, we are forced to be open to the fact that the universe is not all there is.

But, this kind of Creator—timeless, spaceless, immaterial, not made of energy—is exactly what Jews and Christians have believed in for centuries. And they believed this centuries before we had any scientific evidence of that truth. The belief in a Creator is simply the best explanation for *why* there is something rather than nothing.

And if you believe the universe just popped into existence from nothing, then we certainly don't agree. In other words, at bare minimum, I'd say that the universe was caused or created from something, even though we don't know what it is. I could never say that it came from nowhere for no reason.

[Long pause.]

"You know, some scientists argue that 'if you add up the binding (attractive) energy of gravitational attraction, which is negative, and the rest of the whole mass of the universe, which is positive, you get almost zero. No energy, then would be required to create the universe, and therefore no creator is required.'"[10]

> Adding up the amount of positive mass and the negative energy of gravity to zero does not mean that no creator is required. Moreover, what difference does it make in this discussion if "no energy would be required to create the universe"? No one is suggesting God used energy to create the universe. That is, no one who believes in a Creator God believes He used *prior-existing* energy to create the universe. So, this point is irrelevant.
>
> Or, let me give an analogy. Imagine I have a swimming pool full of water and I move all the water one bucket at a time to my neighbor's pool, so that by the end, my pool is empty (negative), but the water is in another pool (positive). Are you telling me that there is no cause for the water in the first place because the amount of water from start to finish equals zero? This is a numbers game that never answers the questions of *why the universe exists at all* and *why it formed the way it did.*[11]

"OK. You say, 'God did it.' Then why not just say, 'Zeus did it'?"

> We could. Now, do we have any religion that tells us these are the characteristics of Zeus? No. The Greeks didn't think he was the all-powerful, immaterial Creator God. Zeus was just one child of many children born from Chronos and Rhea. The Greeks' greatest, original gods, Gaia (goddess of earth) and Uranus (god of the sky) are nothing like the God of the ancient Hebrews. So, that won't work either. The same is true with every single god ever invented (including the Hindu creator god, Brahma, who was born from the genderless force, Brahman). The only Creator God that could be described with these attributes is Yahweh. We just went from millions of god down to one, monotheistic God. That was easy! Now, of course Jews, Christians, and Muslims understand God differently. However, they all agree that there is only one Creator God, and that rules out millions of other gods very easily.

"Well, even if I grant that, how have you not trapped yourself into this infinite regression of the question, 'Who created God' forever? Do you understand what I'm asking? If you're arguing that the universe needs a creator, then who created the Creator?"

I'm so glad you brought this up. I have a few comments about this question.

Professor John Lennox makes two very important points regarding this issue in his debates. First, many scientists fantasize about discovering the "Theory of Everything"—a scientific formula that ties together the four basic forces in the universe (such as String Theory). If we were able to discover that theory, no scientist on the planet would then turn around and ask, "Well then . . . where did this Theory of Everything come from? Huh?" The whole assumption is that once we find the Theory, *no one will challenge its origin because it will be assumed that we have reached rock bottom reality.* There would be nothing to explain because we have reached the fundamental explanation for the universe.

Now, Christians believe this Creator God is like the Theory of Everything: He is the Ground of Being. Of course no one thinks God is a scientific formula. I'm only comparing the *explanatory power* of the Theory of Everything and God. Just like the laws of mathematics exist *by their very nature* (that is, they are not caused by anything material or by energy), so does God exist by His very nature.

Yet, it needs to be asked of scientists: Why is it so easy to believe in a *theory* that needs no causal explanation, but they can't believe in a *God* that needs no causal explanation? I know . . . I know . . . it's because laws are not entities. And since materialists still think that God must be made of matter or energy, they can't get past the fact that a material god must have a material cause. They'd much rather believe in a mathematical formula—even though formulas are not made of matter or energy!—than a *God* who is not made of matter or energy. This strikes me as unnecessarily unfair and close-minded.

Second, as John Lennox often mentions in debates, it works both ways. Theists are always asked, "Then who created your Creator?" If it must be asked of those who believe in a Creator God, then it must be asked of those who believe in a "Creator" *universe* (or for Hawking, "Creator" *gravity*). As Lennox says, since materialists believe that the universe created them, then I am forced to ask them, "If the universe created you, then who created the universe?"

Third, this entire question is irrelevant. Let's assume that the Creator God had parents, and we have no idea who His parents are. This doesn't mean that the Creator God didn't create the universe.

One day you and I walk into my kitchen and see this round, orange thing with silver lining on the counter. It smells good. We analyze its chemical composition, taste it, and decide (really when we first saw it!) that this is not a random accident or caused by quantum fluctuations. We call it a "pumpkin pie." I say aloud, "Wow. This thing is great. I wonder who made it?" And you say to me, "Why in the world would you say that? Tell me this: then who made the pie-maker?" I respond that I have no idea if the pie-maker had parents. "Ah-ha!" you respond, "Therefore, since you can't tell me who the pie-maker's parents are, you shouldn't say that someone made this pie."

Does that seem rational to you?

"No, David, that analogy doesn't work because if you told me that the pie-maker was eternal and uncaused, I'd look at you crazy. I would say, 'Why say that? Shouldn't we assume *first* that the pie-maker is material, like we are?'"

Yes, we should assume the pie-maker is material because we know that there are *material causes for pies*. But remember, we're talking about creating a universe, not a pie. That is, it's the *nature* of the thing being created that allows that option. To say it another way: I know that humans can make pies, and humans are composed of matter and temporal. If someone created the universe, it means whoever or whatever created the universe is outside of time and immaterial (since both came into existence at the Big Bang).

Second, all three monotheistic religions believe that the Creator God who exists is uncaused. That is, they all believe that it has been revealed to them that God is the Uncreated One. He is the Prime Reality.

63

"But why can't the universe just exist? If God doesn't need an explanation, then why can't the universe need no explanation?"

Good questions. Concerning God: God doesn't need a causal explanation outside of Himself because God, by very definition, is uncaused. It's the very definition of an all-powerful Creator God. So, God's existence *does* have an explanation: His nature "explains" His existence.[12]

Concerning the universe: There is no reason at all to assume that the basic particles—the building blocks of the universe—*must exist the way they do by definition*. They could have been different particles.

"Why not?"

Are you suggesting that the particles that make up the universe, quarks and protons and so on, *could not have been any other way*? Our universe couldn't have been made with some other particles we could've called "Lady Gagas" or "shnumeles"? That is, the particles that exist *must exist* by their very nature?

"Sure."

OK . . . I don't know of any reason to believe that the particles that exist that comprise our universe are *necessary* facts.

Do you think anything else in the universe *must exist the way it does*? That is, are there other self-explained phenomena in the universe? And I mean things made of matter or energy.

"No. . . I don't think so."

Oh. So, why do the basic particles of the universe get that privilege? Why the exception?

"Because the universe is different."

In what way? The universe is made of basic particles put in different shapes and forms. Why do you think the particles don't need any causal explanation?

"I just do."

OK. Well, I don't see why. If something is made of matter or energy, as basic particles are, then I see no reason *not* to ask, "Where did it come from?"

"But see, David, this is where these answers sound like a cop-out—a lazy explanation. I understand when Richard Dawkins gets so mad: 'Well, God did it. And God needs no explanation because God is outside all this.' Well, what an incredible evasion of the responsibility to explain. Scientists don't do that. Scientists say, 'We're working on it. We're struggling to understand.'"[13]

That's partly true. But, this is where Dawkins is being so hypocritical. I guarantee that as an evolutionary biologist, Dawkins is *not* "working on it, struggling to understand" how life evolved and came to the appearance of being designed. He's been settled on that issue for most of his life. He has, in his mind, found the most likely explanation for why life looks designed: random mutations acting on natural selection. He has stopped with the theory of evolution. For him, it's the dead end of scientific explanation for the development of life.

To quote him against himself, "Well, all you need to say is, 'Evolution did it.' Well, what an incredible evasion of the responsibility to explain, Dawkins! All you've managed to do is believe in an evolution-of-the-gaps. Why in the world have you just given up? Are you not a scientist?"

"But, he's found the thing that makes the most sense of the data."

So have I. And His name is "God." My point is: once we've found what we think best explains the data, there is no reason at all to *keep looking for alternate explanations*. It is incredibly unfair to think that whenever I think God is the best explanation for something,

I've given up rational thinking and am only committing a god-of-the-gaps reasoning. I could say the same thing about every other explanation for something: the big bang-of-the-gaps or the evolution-of-the-gaps. If we could get past all of the nonsense rhetoric, we're both trying to argue for the cause with the most explanatory power and scope.

It was interesting how the debate between Dawkins and Collins concluded back in 2006. Dawkins said that the right approach to the questions of origins is simply to say we don't know. The interviewer of *Time* magazine asked him if the answer to the origin of the universe could be God—that is, is it in the realm of possibility that God could be the answer to the problem? Dawkins replied, "There could be something incredibly grand and incomprehensible and beyond our present understanding," to which Francis Collins said, "That's God."

Of course, Dawkins didn't like that answer either: "Yes. But it could be any of a billion Gods. It could be God of the Martians or of the inhabitants of Alpha Centauri. The chance of its being a particular God, Yahweh, the God of Jesus, is vanishingly small—at the least, the onus is on you to demonstrate why you think that's the case."[14]

To which I would say, "Absolutely right!" It is certainly the responsibility of any religion to make compelling arguments for its belief in a particular god. That's exactly what we Christians think can be done. At least, finally, Dawkins admitted that "God" could conceivably be an answer to the question of origin.[15] It's a step in the right direction!

"But we need an explanation, or at least, a causal explanation for everything that happens."

Not for first causes, we don't. Remember, as scientists and philosophers have noted for centuries, every material thing in our universe is contingent, that is, it exists because it was caused by something else. For the chain of causal events to begin, there must have been something that first began the whole show. For example, if I saw a billion dominoes, each one falling on the next one, the dominoes couldn't go back forever or they would have never begun falling. Something had to knock over the *very first* domino. God is the Creator of the universe, which means He *set into motion* the entire chain of causal events. And if you think first, uncaused causes need a cause, then you misunderstand what a *first* cause is.[16]

On top of this, we're not talking about what happens *in the universe* when we're talking about God. God is, by definition, He who is *outside of* nature. This is metaphysics. Even *if* God were caused by something else in the supernatural realm, what we know for certain is, it could *not have been a material cause.*

"But what if God were caused by something outside the universe?"

So, now we're speculating on whether or not a God you don't even believe in has a parent, and if so, how that parent caused God to come into existence. [Laughing] This is the definition of speculative. I imagine next we're gonna' talk about whether or not fairies ever dream about unicorns.

"But you think unicorns might exist!"

[Laughs] That's right! They sure might.

"In any case, don't you think that it's convenient that God doesn't need a cause?"

What does convenience have to do with anything?

Oh wait . . . do you believe that monotheists fabricated the belief in an uncaused God in order to respond to recent challenges by new atheists?

"I don't know . . . I've never really thought about it like that before."

Yeah, we need to be clear. This belief has been around for several thousand years. Where did the Jews get it from? It was revealed to them.

Now, this is no small point. No other ancient person would have made such a thing up. It is amazing that the ancient Jews, as a whole, never worshipped the sun or moon or stars or the planet or animals or plants. *All* other ancient cultures did in various degrees. Yet, standing alone among all ancient peoples, the Jews argued that there was one God and that God was the Creator of all that we see, not a part of creation itself. They were very adamant about this point, and this belief is unheard of in the ancient world.

If you want to dismiss the belief in an *uncaused* God, fine. But, at least realize that this is no novel belief; the belief in an uncaused God is at least three or four thousand years old. It was not made up to counter modern objections to Christianity.

"I think it's charming that you Christians attempt to use scientific advancements in your arguments. If this were 100 years ago, you wouldn't be making these arguments. You'd be arguing for the necessity of faith or whatever."[17]

[Laughing] What possible difference does this make? Evidence is evidence. If you were a judge, and an attorney were to come into court one morning and say, "Your Honor, we have newly discovered evidence that greatly helps our case," would you say, "Well, isn't that charming. It's cute how you think you can use new evidence for your case"?

CHAPTER FIVE

Scientific facts that point to God: The universe knew we were coming

On top of all this, the universe from the very beginning has numerous, extremely fine-tuned constants and quantities that allow life—any form of life whatsoever—to exist. Of course, if these constants didn't exist, we wouldn't be here to talk about it. Nevertheless, they *are here* and there is no scientific explanation for why they are here.

Astrophysicist Hugh Ross has listed *ninety-three* constants and inter-related forces that are necessary for life to exist, and his list keeps growing.[1] Here is a small sample of that list: the strong nuclear force constant, the weak nuclear force constant, the gravitational force constant, the electromagnetic force constant, the ratio of electromagnetic force constant to gravitational force constant, the ratio of proton to electron mass, the ratio of number of protons to number of electrons, the ratio of proton to electron charge, the expansion rate of the universe, the mass density of the universe, the baryon (proton and neutron) density of the universe, and we could list about *eighty* more.

I recognize that this topic is huge. I know we can't go into much detail. But just to give you an idea of how "fine-tuned" these can be, the ratio of the electromagnetic force constant to the gravitational force constant cannot be changed by only 1 part in 10^{40}![2] Or, we could talk about how the mass density and space energy density must be fine-tuned to support life. The mass density couldn't be changed 1 part in 10^{60}, and the value of the space energy density couldn't be changed by one part in 10^{120}! These numbers are too enormous to comprehend. To see how huge this number is, there are only about 10^{80} atoms in the entire universe![3]

Fred Hoyle, an atheist astronomer, was doing research on a

particular nuclear reaction called the triple-alpha process, which generates carbon. He discovered the energy level of carbon must be at an extremely precise amount in order for carbon to be created.[4] If it was moved the slightest bit either way, no carbon would form anywhere in the universe. He said that this fact left his atheism "greatly shaken." In fact this is what he admitted:

"Would you not say to yourself, 'Some super-calculating intellect must have designed the properties of the carbon atom, otherwise the chance of my finding such an atom through the blind forces of nature would be utterly minuscule.' Of course you would . . . A common sense interpretation of the facts suggests that a superintellect has monkeyed with physics, as well as with chemistry and biology, and that there are no blind forces worth speaking about in nature. The numbers one calculates from the facts seem to me so overwhelming as to put this conclusion almost beyond question."[5] He's right.

Forget about the universe. What is the likelihood that we would discover one planet with all the necessary conditions for life (again, not just human life, but any life)? Hugh Ross calculated that we need forty-one characteristics of our solar system in order for any life to exist. If you assume, at the most extreme, that our universe has as many planets as it does stars, which it probably doesn't, "that still leaves us with less than one chance in a billion trillion that you'd find even one planet in the entire universe with the capacity for supporting life."[6]

"It's also highly improbable for someone to win the lottery, but someone has to win it."

That's right for the lottery. But the lottery is not an accurate analogy for the fine-tuning of the universe. Here's why: in a lottery, the random number chosen must be chosen because (1) every single person has a number, which means one person must be a winner, and (2) the computer randomly chooses a number that has already been given out. However, there is only one universe and the right "number" does not need to be given out to the universe.

So, imagine a million people buying a lottery ticket for $10 each. That's a jackpot of ten million dollars. And every single person playing has a chance to win because when the computer picks a number, it's a random number which exists on one of the one million tickets given out. Assuming no one loses his or her ticket, there is a guaranteed winner somewhere in the crowd. This is not like our universe.

Here is an accurate analogy for our universe. Imagine the same million people pay $10 not for a ticket, but just to have their name and phone number entered into a drawing. So, a million people pay $10 each, which means there is a jackpot of ten million dollars. One day, you get a call from the lottery office saying that of all the million people who played, you are the only one who has a chance to win the money. At the lottery office they make this clear: "Here's the deal. First, you are the only one who can win the money. No one else among the million people have a chance to win the money. Secondly, our computer has calculated ninety-three different numbers for various physical constants and ratios that are necessary for life to exist. So, to win the money, you need to pick a hundred numbers, one at a time. The first number you randomly pick must be the right number between one and a trillion trillion trillion trillion trillion trillion trillion trillion (that's the fine tuning of just one of the anthropic constants). If you pick the right number, you win it all. If not, we kill every living thing on the planet. If you pick the right number, you'll have to do it again. In fact, you'll have to pick the right number again and again ninety-two more times, and each time the number will be changed by the computer. If at any time you don't pick the right number, we kill everyone."

"Wow!"

It's just virtually impossible that you would pick even one number needed to survive! And even if you did get one right, I would never ever believe that you picked that number by random chance. Ever. The exact same is true for the universe. There is only one universe and the universe which exists had to pick almost a hundred numbers (as far as we know so far) against astronomical odds.

[Long pause.]

"Still, just because we're alive doesn't mean anything special. We're just alive in a universe that supports us."

I still disagree. I'll adapt a well-known analogy by John Leslie. Imagine a hundred snipers aiming right at you. They all fire at you but none of them kill you. After you pass out from shock because you're still alive, you say to your friend, "Can you believe that! Out of all hundred snipers, *none of them killed me!* Surely they never intended on killing me, or they changed their minds, or this is a miracle!" Then your friend responds, "No, no. Listen. You're alive. That's all that matters. It's not special at all. There was always a chance that a hundred highly trained snipers would miss you."

[Laughs]

Again, you'd have *every* right to assume that you were *meant* to live.

"You know, I just can't understand how you can appeal to improbability when the existence of God is just as improbable, if not more.[8] That is, if it is so improbable that a finely-tuned universe had a spontaneous creation out of nothing, then surely God's existence must be just as improbable!"

Yeah, I hear you. Except God's existence can't be judged probable or improbable based on what happens *in the universe*. We're talking about metaphysics, not about what happens in the universe. You're committing a logical fallacy called a "category error."

Remember, no one is arguing for a Super Alien in the Sky. The Creator God we believe in is not just another creature in the universe. We're arguing for a Creator God that is metaphysical or supernatural. If there is a supernatural realm, how could you possibly know what is probable or improbable *there*? We would have to know about the laws—if there are any—of the supernatural realm in order to make claims of probability. Therefore, the degree of probability must be determined *by what happens in the supernatural realm*, not by our realm.

"You know, you were mentioning how there is only one universe. I thought scientists believe we are just one universe among millions or trillions of universes. It's called the Multiverse Theory or something like that. If there are millions of universes, then we could just be in the one that has the right conditions."

Yeah, I know what you're talking about. I have a few reflections about this.

First, there is not a shred of evidence for this theory. None. In fact, as general relativity demonstrates, *even if* other universes did exist, the boundaries of those universes would never intersect with our own. So, no matter how much anyone ever argues for other universes, there will never be a time in the history of humanity that we could ever test the hypothesis. This doesn't sound too promising for a scientific explanation.

I think the eminent quantum theorist, John Polkinghorne, says it well: "Let us recognize these speculations for what they are. They are not physics, but in the strictest sense, metaphysics. There is no purely scientific reason to believe in an ensemble of universes. By construction these other worlds are unknowable by us. A possible explanation of equal intellectual respectability—and to my mind greater economy and elegance—would be that this one world is the way it is, because it is the creation of the will of a Creator who purposes that it should be so."[9]

Secondly, having other universes *still doesn't answer the question* of why our universe is fine-tuned for life in the first place.

"Well, cosmologists have several models for the universe, such as the inflationary model which says our universe might be one of many that are bubbling up from a primitive quantum fluctuation."

That's right. And none of them explain away the fact that our universe has fine-tuning for life. All of these theories presuppose an initial fine-tuned "universe maker" mechanism. This just delays the problem. If our universe received its fine-tuning from this initial inflation, where *did that initial inflation receive its fine-tuning?*

Third, appealing to other *hypothetical* universes commits what's known as the "gambler's fallacy." I'll adapt an analogy from Astrophysicist Hugh Ross.[10] Do you have a coin?

[Pulls out a quarter.]

OK. Imagine you flip this coin ten thousand times and every single time you get heads. In utter amazement, you reflect on the fact that your quarter has landed on heads for ten thousand flips! You stare at the quarter, thinking *surely* there must be something unique about *this* quarter that would cause this to happen.

Then, I say, "Nah, nah. Listen. Let's assume that out in the world today there are $2^{10,000}$ quarters that *might possibly exist*. Let's also assume that all of *those* coins were also flipped ten thousand times. Let's also assume that flipping all of those other quarters produced different results. Therefore, let's just conclude that your quarter just happened to be one of possible instances where it's possible to land on heads ten thousand times in a row. Therefore, there's still a 50/50 chance that your quarter will land on tails. I'll bet you on it."

This is the gambler's fallacy.

"So the fallacy is in the probability that the quarter will land on tails based on several assumptions of what's happening *outside* with hypothetical quarters?"

That's right. First, there is *no evidence* at all that there *must* be $2^{10,000}$ quarters outside the café. Secondly, there is no evidence that the hypothetical quarters outside have been flipped ten thousand consecutive times. Finally, there is no evidence that the results from flipping those hypothetical quarters outside are different from your quarter.

So it is with other hypothetical universes. If there is no evidence of any other universes, no evidence of how they are configured, and no evidence that their configuration is different from our own universe, then there is no reason to assume *anything* about our universe as it compares to hypothetical universes.

Back to my analogy: since you only had evidence of your coin, you would be right to assume something was rigged. The same is true of the universe.

Now, the reason why I don't believe in multiple universes is because there is no evidence for it. It bears no threat to my belief that God is Creator. If there are millions of universes, we're only delaying the problem: where did *millions of universes* come from?

"The fact that there are highly precise conditions in the universe does not mean that God exists."

Right. No one can say logically, "The odds of the universe being formed in the way it was is nearly impossible, therefore God exists." I'm just convinced that no open-minded person could learn of all these facts and not immediately assume it was *designed* to be the way it is. Like with the snipers allowing me to live, we have reason to assume our life-permitting universe was intentionally designed.

Do you see this? This is no small point: we all agree in the scientific facts, the evidence. *How we interpret the facts* is determined *by our worldview*. This is why worldview is so important. It forces us to be open or closed to certain conclusions. And since I'm not a materialist, when I consider the overwhelming amount of fine-tuned constants and quantities that are necessary for a life-permitting universe, the most logical conclusion I make for the origin of "rigging" is a "Rigger."

Moreover, Judaism and Christianity have been arguing for centuries that a universe designed for life is exactly the kind of universe we should expect. That is, the God that Christians believe in is rational, orderly, and wants life in our universe. So, we *expect to find* these kinds of constants and quantities that support life.

"I was reading from the scholarly world of YouTube comments and came across the argument you seem to be making. The person was so ticked off at 'religious people' making this argument: 'If it was any other way, we wouldn't be here to judge it in the first place, it's mind-bendingly obvious. The universe isn't the way it is for us, we are the way we are so we can inhabit it. We evolved eyes because the sun radiates light which allow us to see, the sun didn't start radiating light to make our eyes useful. The stupidity and backward thinking is excruciating.' I don't see how you could get out of this problem."

Isn't this another great example of congeniality? I'm a little unclear how calling people "stupid and backward thinking" helps the conversation. Of course, that's assuming people like him or her even want to have conversations.

"Hey, I can give you examples of religious people saying some hateful things!"

Fair enough. And Christians, at least, should know better!
Anyway, I didn't ask you why human life is able *to be sustained by* the universe; I asked you *why* the universe has these constants in the first place. This pleasant person has utterly missed the point.
Imagine I've never been in water before. When I see a river, I jump in and grab a small raft and begin floating. I say to you, "Wow! Look; I'm floating! Why do you think I'm able to float like this?"
You respond, "Your stupidity and backward thinking is excruciating. It infuriates me to no end. If you weren't *in* the river you wouldn't be here to judge what floating means in the first place."
"Of course not," I respond. "What does that have to do with my question at all?" I'm not asking *how is it that I now know what floating feels like*, I'm asking, "Why is water and this raft able to hold my body up? Who or what fine-tuned the laws of buoyancy in order for this to happen?"

"So in your analogy, do you think the laws of buoyancy were designed just so you could float? Or, do you believe the sun began emitting light millions of years ago just so your eyes can see?"

Well, wait a second. The belief that the sun was designed with me in mind and the belief that human life developed in response to the sun are most certainly *not* mutually exclusive beliefs.

As a Christian, I think both are true because they came from the same mind. If a young person walked into my classroom and saw all the tables and chairs in a particular order, the white board and projector, and my desk, they would immediately assume that this is a classroom, that this room is deliberately designed with them in mind. And these tables and chairs could have been here for millions of years before they ever walked in. It might be a really selfish thought to assume it was designed with them in mind, but nevertheless, it would certainly be a rational inference.

The only way to know if something was designed for a particular purpose is to ask the one who designed it, like the sun in your example. There is no reason to suppose that God did *not* design the sun with us in mind, or at least the fact that the universe would produce stars, even though it's been radiating heat energy for millions of years.

My wife and I prepared a baby's room almost a year in advance to our child inhabiting that room. I imagine you would have said to our baby, "You mean to tell me that you think that this whole room was designed with you in mind *a whole year before you even existed*?! Isn't it much more likely that the reason you sleep in a crib and play with those toys is because that's just how you naturally adapted to your environment?"

Or, let's imagine that my wife and I first move into a house, years before we have children. I plant a tree so that one day our children will be able to play on it. It grows for years according to an *undirected, natural process* so that one day, years later, I attach a swing. We then have children and wait several more years for them to get to the age where they can swing. My son grows up, plays on its branches and swings on its swing. Is my child "stupid and backwards thinking" to think that the tree was planted with him in mind so many years before he existed? Are we really forced into the false alternatives of *either* the tree was planted with my son in mind *or* my son adapted to the tree as he grew?

This seems absurd. If there is no God, then yes, there is no purpose or design. If there is a God, of course the universe could be our "baby room." Of course the universe could be our "tree to swing on." Of course God could have designed it with us in mind, even if God used natural processes to achieve His purposes in His design.

In any case, the question remains: "Where did all of the multiple, extremely improbable fine-tuning constants come from in the first place?" Even if there are billions of other universes, it's *much more likely* that our universe wouldn't have the necessary conditions. The odds are just too staggering. I concur with the atheist Hoyle: someone's been "monkeying" with things, and this "monkeying" is *necessary* for galaxies, stars, and even life.

"But David, when you look at the size of the universe, doesn't it seem arrogant to you that you think human life is the goal?"

This is a common assumption that is erroneous. Just because the fine-tuning of the universe allows for life, it doesn't mean it's arrogant to admit that fact. It reminds of something Stephen Hawking said to Diane Sawyer: "[People who believe in God have] made [God] a human-like being with whom one can have a personal relationship. When you look at the vast size of the universe and how insignificant and accidental human life is in it, that seems most impossible."[11] Everything about this statement is nonsensical.

First, we didn't *make* a human-like being out of God. This is called "begging the question" in logic. It's where you assume your conclusion is true, rather than demonstrate that it's true. As usual, atheists *assume* God doesn't exist and then make excuses why people would believe something false. It's the typical, "Well, we know God doesn't exist. But they think he does, so they fashioned a god in whom they can believe." I could just as easily *assume* that atheism is false and then deduce that Hawking is an atheist because he just doesn't want to believe in someone smarter than he is.

Secondly, what possible difference could it make that the universe is vast? Does Hawking really think that *size* determines value or worth? He must think that the average basketball player is far more

SCIENTIFIC FACTS THAT POINT TO GOD: THE UNIVERSE KNEW WE WERE COMING

valuable than he is. Moreover, in what way does the universe's *vastness* contradict the existence of God or the fact that God is personal? This is logically incoherent.

He's also assuming life is insignificant and accidental, which is "begging the question." Yet, if you're an atheist, as he is, of course life is insignificant and accidental. Life has no objective purpose at all.

[Laughing] "Are you telling me that you think atheists can't have meaningful lives?"

On a subjective level, sure they can. Scientists, rapists, historians, pedophiles, businesswomen, gangsters, politicians: most people think their lives have meaning. That is, most people think they have a purpose in life because they are completing a task, receiving pleasure, or even doing some good. But on a materialistic worldview, none of these things are what I would call *really* significant. Some might say "objectively" significant instead of *really* significant.

"Now wait! If I were to spend my entire life working on curing cancer, and found a cure, my life would certainly be significant and have purpose!"

I concur. If you were to cure cancer, you would alleviate pain and suffering, and that would help people. That's right.

"Right."

But in the long run, really, this is all insignificant. If life is "accidental" and "insignificant" (as Hawking said) then there is no objective value to life. We might *enjoy* certain things; we might feel passionately about certain causes; we might do some good for people. But in the end, those feelings of worth and value are illusory.[12] If there is no God, we are temporary cosmic accidents. We barely made it into existence and we will certainly be destroyed in the future as our sun explodes or expands and burns up the planet. After that comes the long, cold, dark emptiness of space as all the energy in the universe is spent. What possible difference does your life make if that's the ultimate destiny of all humans? If atheism is true, once you die, you're done. As soon as your memory dies off among family and friends—and it will certainly die off—you will no longer exist in any form at all.

"Who cares about the 'long term'? Why can't we just focus on the good we do now?"

Well, we can. But for many—and I know it's true for me—it's demoralizing to think about how our absolute greatest achievements in life are, in the long-run, not really significant.[13]

"How can you say that?"

If I built a dam that blocked water from destroying a village, it would be a great good. I've managed to help save an entire village of people. But then, a great rain comes twenty-seven years later, breaks the dam, and the entire village drowns. Now, building the dam was significant, and for those at the time, they might have said it was *really* significant. But no one *after* the flood would suggest that the dam was really significant after all because the dam didn't last. It didn't work in the long-term. Everyone died. And that's the point I'm making. I believe that *real* significance, or someone might say, "objective" significance comes from its ability to make a difference long-term. If we all die in the end anyway, what *real* possible significance do our achievements have?

"Well, they matter to me."

I know it's common to *act* like things really matter. If you do, then you're not alone. Remember how Stephen Hawking said that all life is "accidental" and "insignificant"? I was quite surprised to hear Stephen Hawking tell Diane Sawyer in the same interview—the one where he just said that life is "accidental" and "insignificant"—that he offers three pieces of advice to his children: "One, remember to look up at the stars and not down at your feet. Two, never give up work. Work gives you meaning and purpose and life is empty without it," he said. "Three, if you are lucky enough to find love, remember it is there and don't throw it away."[14]

"What's wrong with that?"

If I were Hawking's child, and I were being logically consistent with Hawking's beliefs, I might respond (with due respect):

"What scientific evidence do you have that we *ought* to 'look up at the stars' instead of our 'feet'? I need scientific proof before I decide if this is the most rational choice for me to make. And why are the stars more important than my feet? Are you suggesting the universe is more important than I am? Why? What evidence leads you to that conclusion?

"Also, you can't really think that you have any moral authority to place that obligation upon me if what you are saying is merely the product of blind, evolutionary, survival instincts thrust upon you by your ancestors. Just give it time: eventually the chemical reactions in your brain will produce different thoughts. I think I'll wait until I hear what else you are determined to think and say to me by random, non-rational, cerebral accidents occurring in your brain.

"Oh yeah, how and in what way does work 'give you meaning and purpose' if we are 'insignificant accidents' of the cosmos? I know, Daddy, that you might *enjoy* work, but that doesn't mean it has any real, objective purpose. What possible meaning and purpose could you get from a job that will end in total destruction and entropy, once the universe grows too cold for life? Do you think that a child's sand castle by the ocean has objective purpose? I know you think that you are giving humans some understanding of how the cosmos work. So what? Your findings are utterly insignificant since you are just one small speck on a random planet in the cosmos. All of your achievements will be inconsequential once all humans die. And on top of that, your ideas can't be trusted anyway since there is no way to know they are true because your scientific observations are just random biochemical accidents driven by your survival instincts. Right?

"Finally, what is 'love' but random biochemical reactions in my brain caused by my evolutionary need to procreate and propagate the *homo sapiens* species? What is the scientific evidence that 'love' exists? I need proof, Daddy. And if this instinct called 'love' is merely determined by evolution, then why do you need to tell me that I *ought* not to 'throw it away'? What possible choice do I have in the matter if evolution has determined what I think and feel? And Daddy, isn't it much better *not* to stay trapped to being in love, but to have sex with as many females as possible so that I can propagate our species?"

"Wow."

[Takes a drink.]

CHAPTER SIX

Scientific facts that point to God: The origin of life

"So what about those other reasons you gave me?"

Yeah. The origin of life. There are several reasons why it is extremely improbable that life arose from non-life by random, accidental chance.[1] You must have functional amino acids in order to form functional, self-replicating proteins. You must have functional, self-replicating proteins to have living cells and living organisms.

So here's the deal: (1) Scientists seem certain that environmental conditions on Earth billions of years ago were most hostile to amino acids forming. It is highly unlikely that those *primitive environmental conditions* allowed amino acids to form in the first place. The atmosphere would have been composed of various gases that would have attacked the cells immediately. (2) Even if amino acids somehow assembled, there are a host of *chemicals* that would have been hostile to amino acids. (3) It is highly unlikely that the amino acids formed in the precise chains necessary to form peptides by random chance. (4) Amino acids and sugars come in mirror images of each other, but living things only have L amino acids and D sugars. "How could we possibly get one hundred or more amino acids that are all Ls from a mixture of equal concentrations of Ls and Ds? This problem has been studied extensively but the explanation remains elusive."[2] (5) Finally, the only way that amino acids know how to form into the exact three-dimensional shapes necessary to form functional proteins is by genetic information, called DNA (RNA has a similar function). Statistically, the odds of finding just one functional protein by chance are 1 out of 10^{164}![3] I can't even imagine such a large number: a ten followed with one hundred sixty-four zeroes. And this number is *twice* as big as the amount of particles in the entire universe! Not only is this figure staggering, these odds are for just *one* functioning protein. It takes between 250 and 400 proteins to form a single-cell organism!

DNA is genetic information; it's software code. And there is tons of it in the most basic life. "The origin of the large amount of information in DNA that is expressed in the amazing molecular complexity essential for life is the central enigma of the origin of life."[4]

Bacteria is the smallest living organism we know of. E. coli bacteria has the equivalent of eight hundred pages of information.[5] Eight hundred pages! Richard Dawkins says the message found in just the cell nucleus of a tiny amoeba has over 2000 pages of information, and the entire amoeba has over 2,000,000 pages![6]

"Wow! That's a lot."

[Long pause.]

"But, just because we don't know how life started doesn't mean God did it. I can hear Richard Dawkins say, 'But why give up now with lazy thinking? We're struggling to find out how this all happened.' There are working theories of how it all began."

Yes, scientists are working on theories, such as the "metabolic replicator" theory or assuming that RNA came first. Yet, all of them are *far* from being close to an explanation. Each theory has huge obstacles.

Again, it's not "giving up" or "lazy thinking" to think that you've found the most rationally-satisfying answer to a problem. But, I do appreciate what Francis Collins says about this. He warns against a "god-of-the-gaps" process, where we give God the credit for something we just don't know yet. Collins states: "If God's intention in creating the universe was to lead to creatures with whom He might have fellowship, namely human beings, and if the complexity required to start the process of life was beyond the ability of the universe's chemicals to self-assimilate, couldn't God have stepped in to initiate the process? This could be an appealing hypothesis, given that no serious scientist would currently claim that a naturalistic explanation for the origin of life is at hand. But that is true today, and it may not be true tomorrow."[7]

He finds it safer to assume God is the origin of "mathematical principles and order in creation," since those are known facts.[8] I concur with him.

Yet, the situation Collins described for life is *precisely* the thing that would require a divine intervention. If it *is* true, as he said, that "the complexity required to start the process of life was *beyond the ability of the universe's chemicals to self-assimilate,*" what other possible option is there? That is, if the *universe* couldn't do it, then what else is an option? Saying aliens dropped off life or a comet brought it a few billion years ago (this theory is called "panspermia") doesn't answer the question at all if the *universe* isn't capable of producing the first complex life. So, the question is: is it possible for the *universe* to produce incredibly complex life from non-living chemicals? There is no apparent reason to answer in the affirmative.

So, there are three reasons why I think God is the best causal explanation for the origin of life and DNA/RNA. First, it is so overwhelmingly improbable that complex living organisms with genetic information originated from non-rational, non-living chemicals due to the reasons given above.

Second, DNA/RNA is genetic *information*, and I don't know of any non-rational process that can produce *rational* information. I don't see how we can get past the fact that information always comes from an intelligence or mind.

Third, it's not difficult to imagine . . .

"But wait a second: you're positing a more complex creature for such simple things. Why invoke something so much more complex like a divine mind? Shouldn't we be looking for simpler explanations? You know, Ockham's Razor."

Well first, I'm not sure why simplicity should be treated as the chief scientific criterion for truth. I think the best way to reach conclusions is to ask the question, "What do I find most compelling?" Or, "Which cause explains the most of what we observe?" not, "What is the best explanation, as long as it's very simple?" Just let the evidence lead us where it leads us. And this is crucial: We should allow what makes the most sense of the evidence *to form our worldview*. We should *not* make decisions that fit our predetermined worldview. To let our worldview taint how we analyze evidence is to have the tail wag the dog.

Second, if I told you: "Look at this book by N.T. Wright that I'm reading. Would you believe that this simple book full of ink and paper actually comes from one of the best minds Christianity has to offer?"[9] Would you consider it irrational to believe that *information* in the form of a book could not possibly be from a human because that explanation was too complex? Isn't the most rational inference to make when one encounters information is that a mind is the source?

And Ockham's Razor is *not* the principle that everything should be simple. Rather, it's the principle that we should *not multiply causes beyond necessity*. I agree. Multiplying causes for no good reason ought to be avoided.

"Yeah, but that doesn't mean N.T. Wright has no material cause."

That's right. Information only implies an intelligence as the cause. Christians do not believe that information in DNA/RNA points to God being immaterial and timeless; the creation of the universe points to those attributes. Rather, information points to the belief that a superior intelligence created it.

Third, God's mind is not made up of complex moving parts. "As an unembodied mind, God is a remarkably simple entity. . . . Certainly such a mind may have complex ideas (it may be thinking, for example, of the infinitesimal calculus), but the mind itself is a remarkably simple entity."[10]

"So what was the third reason you believe God is the best causal explanation for the origin of life and DNA/RNA?"

Because it's not difficult to imagine God creating life since He created the universe. To me, creating the universe and creating life seems to fit God's "style," much like a mother bird will first build a nest and then place the egg in the nest. This fact seems reinforced by the exact time living organisms were created. Remember, if life had not come into existence at the precise time it did, we wouldn't even be able to study the universe. Astrophysicist Hugh Ross tells us: "If we were created any earlier in cosmic history, the age of the universe would limit our view both in terms of the distance we would look out to and in the numbers and kinds of objects that would have formed. If we were created any later, the space energy density of the universe would have sped an increasingly larger portion of the universe beyond our limits of possible observation."[11] God, apparently, wanted us to be able to see His handiwork. Life was introduced into the cosmic drama at a particular time that allowed us to study the universe. This is amazing.

In the same way that I don't believe a universe can create itself and self-assemble itself with multiple fine-tuned constants, I don't believe life can create itself and self-assemble itself with extreme sophistication and complexity based on self-generated genetic information. Of course, the whole of my Christian faith is not in this belief. If one day a scientist explains it all with materialistic explanations, I'll say, "Cool." I'll be *extremely* surprised, but not one step closer to abandoning Christianity.

Now what happened to life after that is irrelevant to me. I don't have a problem with believing that God designed certain mechanisms that allow life to develop. Of course, even if we fully understood the evolutionary mechanism (which we don't), it doesn't mean that life wasn't designed.

"I don't understand what you mean."

Eminent mathematician John Lennox makes this point all the time in debates. We must not, as Richard Dawkins and other materialists do, confuse *mechanism* with *agency*.

I could bring in the best mechanical engineer, electrical engineer, chemist, plumber, physicist, and geologist to study my house. They could offer a 600-page document that described in detail how all of the plumbing, electrical work, etc., in my house works. If at the end of the document they reported, "Since we know exactly how your house works, we now know that no one designed this house." Wouldn't you consider this nonsense? Understanding how the house works (mechanism) has nothing to do with the question of if, who, or what designed the house (agency).

Let's assume that evolution is correct. In this assumption, we see the evidence and conclude that there is a natural, undirected process, or highly complex mechanism, that develops life. Then, we just stop seeking explanations because we have discovered a highly complex mechanism. But there is no reason to stop there. We then get to ask, What caused the highly complex mechanism?

I like John Lennox's analogy which illustrates the point: "Think of a man who, on seeing a car for the first time, supposes that it is made directly by humans only later to discover it is made in a robotic factory by robots which in turn were made by machines made by humans. His initial inference to intelligent origin was not wrong: it was his concept of the nature of the implementation of that intelligence that was inaccurate. To put it another way, direct human activity was not detectable in the robotic factory because it is the existence of the factory itself and its machines that is, ultimately, the result of intelligent human activity."[12]

So, I believe God is the Designer Agent. At the very least, God designed certain mechanisms that allow life to develop. Yet, I still have serious doubts about how random mutation can produce huge amounts of genetic *information* to produce new species. I also wish that there were more concrete examples of "transitional fossils." Steven Jay Gould, Harvard evolutionary biologist, wished for the same thing:

"The extreme rarity of transitional forms in the fossil record persists as the trade secret of paleontology. The evolutionary trees that adorn our textbooks have data only at the tips and nodes of their branches . . . in any local area, a species does not arise gradually by the gradual transformation of its ancestors; it appears all at once and fully formed."[13]

"OK. I'm sorry; I have got to go to the restroom."

Good call.

CHAPTER SEVEN

More facts that point to God: morality and the soul

[Comes back] "Alright, you said there were five things that pointed to God. What were the last two?"

Morality and the existence of the soul. Let's talk about morality. We've already discussed certain laws that govern the universe, such as the laws of physics and mathematics. There is also a law that governs humans, even though unlike the laws of physics, humans can break or rebel against the Moral Law.

Nearly every person on the planet has always had, as long as history has been recorded, an intuitive sense of right and wrong, a moral compass that is expressed through a series of virtues. That is, there is an Objective Moral Law that declares certain behavior as right and wrong, depending on the situation.

"Like what?"

Well, this might not be exhaustive, but I could mention honesty, justice, fairness, charity, loyalty, kindness, honor or respect, protection of innocent life, helping those in need, courage, and gratitude. Perhaps there are more. Of course, a person doesn't need *to believe* in God to perceive these virtues. Nor are these virtues right in every situation. There are times when we feel it is wrong to enact justice, when the Moral Law tells us to forgive.

In any case, these virtues are objective: they are not personal preferences or tastes. Even though there are times when certain virtues must be overridden by other virtues (such as when the "protection of human life" must be overridden if the protection of one life means many more die), it doesn't mean the virtues become evil or wrong. That is, objective virtues are always objectively right, even though the Moral Law might tell us to choose a particular virtue over another one depending on the situation.

And by objective, I mean transcendent or beyond us all, just like mathematics and logic are transcendent or beyond us all. That is, it doesn't matter what your culture or gender is, 2+2=4. It's universal; it's objective; it's transcendent; it's beyond personal preference. There is no such thing as American math or European logic. Math and logic transcend culture, just like objective morals do.

The same is true about vices. There are some behaviors that are objectively wrong. One might mention genocide. When I say that Hitler's pogroms against the Jews were wrong, I don't mean "I don't prefer it" or "It's against my personal taste that he tried to eradicate an entire race of people." I mean, *it was wrong. It was objectively, morally wrong.* It *was* wrong, would be wrong if it were occurring now, and *will* always be wrong, even if Nazis were still in power. And if there is just one thing that is objectively wrong, then relativism, the belief that morals are just subjective preferences, is false.

"No. We all know that people come to different moral conclusions."

Just because people come to different moral conclusions doesn't mean there aren't right and wrong answers to moral problems. Do you also believe that the laws of mathematics are relative because people don't get the same answer on math tests?

Or, consider this: Around 3-6% of the population suffers from dyscalculia, the mental condition where a person has a neurological problem with understanding numbers and calculations. Because this disorder exists, does that mean mathematics is subjective?

Or, what if we consider the neurological or psychological condition, sociopathy? Sociopaths, those who demonstrate no real awareness of morality, are *considered debilitated.* That is, the exception proves the rule. Being able to demonstrate a small portion of society that doesn't seem to be aware of objective morals does not disprove objective morality.

"What about the fact that different cultures have different morals."

Like I mentioned already, different cultures show a profound similarity in what they consider to be moral. Don't confuse different *expressions* of morality with different morals. The Japanese bow; Europeans kiss both cheeks; Americans shake hands—everyone is expressing honor and respect, objective morals to which every person submits. Imagine a culture where people were praised for being disrespectful, dishonest, disloyal, cowardly, coldhearted, or selfish.

"So what does this prove?"

That as far as we can tell from the history of humanity, humans have believed that certain behavior is considered objectively right or objectively wrong. That is, morality hasn't really changed in centuries. Of course there has been moral progress, that is, we've discovered more about the Moral Law just as we've discovered more about the laws of mathematics throughout history. Secondly, we can see that the entire human race is under a transcendent Moral Law. We all know we ought to do certain things, even though we fail to do them. And if there is a transcendent Moral Law, there simply must be some authority that transcends all humans in order to give this Moral Law. That is, if we call morality, "a commandment for how to behave," then who is the Commander? This "authority that transcends all humans," or "Commander," is what theists call, "God."

"Hmmm . . . Yeah, but, you know in logic, there are rules that humans are supposed to follow. For example, the rule of non-contradiction says that a person couldn't make a self-refuting statement and still *make sense*. One might say that it's a 'commandment' not to be contradictory. Do you believe that God is 'commanding' humans not to be logically contradictory?"

No, I don't for two reasons. First, no one feels compelled to be logical. We certainly do feel compelled to be moral. That is, there is no "oughtness" in logic, while there certainly is in morality. Secondly, what we feel for being immoral is quite different from what we feel when we're illogical. For example, if I say something illogical, I won't feel anything (except a bit embarrassed?). No one feels guilt and shame for making mistakes in mathematics or logic. However, if I do something immoral, then I feel guilt and shame because I know I should have done the moral thing.

"But there are many studies that show how animals, especially primates, have some sort of morality."

First, it must be admitted that the only way to know what an animal is *obligated to do* is by being an animal. If an alien were to observe humans (and not be able to communicate with them), "his observations would only show what we did, and the moral law is about what we ought to do."[1] We might observe animals and make inferences based on their behavior, but we can never know if animals are under the Moral Law because we are not one of them and we cannot communicate with them to find out. I would be interested to ask a chimpanzee, "Do you ever feel guilt? Do you ever feel a moral obligation to suppress an instinct and choose another instinct because one of the instincts you feel is the *good* thing to do in this instance?"

If a lion were to conquer a lioness sexually, no human (and apparently no other animal) would accuse the lion of rape. When a lion hunts and consumes a gazelle, no one castigates the lion for "murdering" the gazelle.[2] Yet, if I were walking down the street and saw a man jump on a woman and have sex with her, no one would look the other way while the man did what his natural instincts "commanded" him to do. We would feel outrage at this immoral act, and if we did not feel outrage, we would feel the need to excuse such behavior. In either case, no one in his right mind would look dispassionately at that event because the man is just doing what's "natural."

Even if animals did perceive the Moral Law, it doesn't mean that the Moral Law doesn't exist. It would only reinforce the fact that the Moral Law is transcendent. Perhaps other animals have some hint of the Moral Law. In any case, Francis Collins is right: "Though other animals may at times appear to show glimmerings of a moral sense, they are certainly not widespread, and in many instances other species' behavior seems to be in dramatic contrast to any sense of universal rightness. It is the awareness of right and wrong, along with the development of language, awareness of self, and the ability to imagine the future, to which scientists generally refer when trying to enumerate the special qualities of *Homo sapiens*."[3]

"But it's been determined that morality came from evolution. Of course we have morals, but they are just instincts or feelings inherited by thousands of generations of primates."

Even if genetics develops our sense of morality, it doesn't mean that objective morals are genetic. It would mean that our ability to apprehend moral values developed. Even if evolution helped us apprehend mathematic facts, mathematic facts would still be objective.

"But isn't morality just an instinct?"

No. Instincts are amoral—that is, morally neutral. Morality cannot be an instinct because morality tells us which instincts to suppress and which instinct to allow. That is, the Moral Law judges between instincts: it tells us which instinct is right and which instinct is wrong, which means the Moral Law cannot simply be an instinct.[4] C.S. Lewis gives the helpful analogy of the Moral Law as being a sheet of music that tells us which notes to play. We can imagine how a piano does not have "two kinds of notes on it, the 'right' notes and the 'wrong' ones. Every single note is right at one time and wrong at another. The Moral Law is not any one instinct or any set of instincts: it is something which makes a kind of tune (the tune we call goodness or right conduct) by directing the instincts."[5]

This is why morality cannot be an instinct. Morality transcends our instincts and tells us which instinct to follow. Morality is not about *what we do*; it is about *what we ought to do*.

Here is another reason why morality is not a result of evolution: if morality is inherited instincts, then "good" and "bad" are illusory. These words should be dropped from our vocabulary. This is a common critique. If our morals were only driven by survival needs, it would also mean that *all of our thoughts* are merely driven by survival needs. This would mean that our morals and thoughts might help us survive, but they might be completely false.[6]

The fact is, evolutionary theories of morality undermine morality. It says, "Your moral sense of being unselfish is really about survival," so go be unselfish with people because "it's the right thing to do." This is logically incoherent. If all of our instincts and behavior were merely the result of survival instincts, then there is no reason to trust any instinct or thought as "the right thing to do" because "the right" does not exist. All morality is just a feeling—a passing one at that.

C.S. Lewis exposes this: "For when men say 'I ought' they certainly think they are saying something, something true, about the nature of the proposed action, and not merely about their own feelings. But if [Materialism] is true, 'I ought' is the same sort of statement as 'I itch' or 'I'm going to be sick.' . . . All moral judgments would be statements about the speaker's feelings, mistaken by him for statements about something else (the real moral quality of actions) which does not exist."[7]

Richard Dawkins tried to convince us in his book, *The Selfish Gene,* that we should ignore what our genes tell us, because our genes instruct us to be selfish. "Be warned that if you wish, as I do, to build a society in which individuals cooperate generously and unselfishly towards a common good, you can expect little help from biological nature. Let us try to teach generosity and altruism, because we are born selfish. Let us understand what our own selfish genes are up to, because we may then at least have the chance to upset their designs, something that no other species has ever aspired to."[8]

I certainly concur that we are born selfish, and that we probably are the only species who has ever "aspired" to be moral. However, I have several responses to Dawkins. First, genes cannot be selfish or unselfish; they are amoral. Antony Flew says it well: "Genes, of course, can be neither selfish nor unselfish any more than they or any other nonconscious entities can engage in competition or make selections."[9] Only human *motives* can be selfish or unselfish.

Second, what makes him think material genes affect our psychological motives? Even if evolution causes our genes to be "selfish," why would this make our motives selfish? This is extreme determinism. Moreover, if all of our motives are determined by our genes, then why trust Richard Dawkins' motives for anything he says and writes? Apparently his genes were telling him to write that book . . . and for selfish, survival reasons, too. And if survival is determining his motives for writing that book, then I have no reason to trust that what he's saying is true. This is why it is nonsense to try, as he says, to attempt to live generously and altruistically. Any such attempt would be futile because our motivations for living "generously" couldn't be trusted to help us at all.

Again, Antony Flew says it well: "No eloquence can move programmed robots. But in fact none of it is true—or even faintly sensible. Genes, as we have seen, do not and cannot necessitate our conduct. Nor are they capable of the calculation and understanding required to plot a course of either ruthless selfishness or sacrificial compassion."[10]

Third, why try to suppress what nature tells us to do if it's gotten us this far? That is, what makes being selfishness wrong if it's Mother Nature's way? It sure seems counterproductive to fight against an undirected, survival mechanism (as he believes) if it's gotten us the human race.

"Oh come on. You don't think it's wrong to be unselfish?"

Of course I do! But I know *why* I do. Again, if being selfish is Mother Nature's way, then *why is it wrong*? As David Hume said over three hundred years ago, this is the naturalistic fallacy: you cannot get a moral *ought* from an *is*. That is, one cannot logically move from something that occurs in nature and make a moral inference. If our genetic nature says to act in a certain way, then it's only natural. You cannot move from "it's natural" to "it's morally right" or "it's morally wrong." Nature is not compelled to obey the Moral Law.

So, really, why not murder and pillage and rape and do whatever I want to do if it helps me survive?

"Because it's . . ."

Wrong? You can't say that if morality is just natural instincts. The only way you can say something is "wrong" or "right" is if *you assume a Moral Law that transcends our instincts.*

"No. I can say that rape is wrong because it hurts the other person."

Why is hurting a person objectively wrong?

"Because the person didn't ask to have sex. She or he was forced."

Why is it wrong to force sex?

"Because humans should have a choice."

Why is having a choice in sex objectively moral?

"Because no one wants to have sex unless there is a choice."

So, something is objectively morally wrong if it violates someone's freedom of choice?

"Yes."

I can't imagine anyone saying—when asked why rape is wrong—that rape is wrong because it violates the person's freedom to choose sex. I think rape is disgusting, nasty, brutal, and evil. The violence and power-mongering it displays is despicable. Of course I concur with you that sex should be freely given, but I don't think that rape is wrong just because it takes away freedom.

But the biggest problem with your criterion is that it disregards nearly every objective moral good we know: honesty, courage, respect, etc. None of these things are good because they respect someone's freedom of choice. Moreover, objective moral vices don't meet your criteria: being rude, ignoring the poor, etc., have nothing to do with freedom of choice.

[Pauses]

"Ahhh . . . Well, you could say that people who rape don't live happy lives because we tend to incarcerate them (unless a family member doesn't kill the rapist first!)."

> Sure, if they get caught. But this doesn't make rape objectively wrong; it makes it against my preference, since in most cases, I wish to survive or not be locked up in a small room.

"So you're telling me that a person can't be moral without God?"

> No. I'm not saying that. Though, there is a particular view among certain Christians that humans cannot, in fact, do anything "good" without God doing it in you, but that's for another conversation. Instead, I'm only suggesting that if you believe there are objective rights and wrongs, I don't know of any possible *grounding* for objective morals unless there is a God.

"But there are all types of ethical systems. I can remember reading Aristotle's *Nicomachean Ethics*. Or what about other ethicists who argue that objective morals are abstract objects not grounded in God?"

> There are different types of ethics. That's right. But none of these systems explain why nearly every human on the planet has similar objective morals. How could this be true if people held to these objective morals before Aristotle existed or if they've never heard of him? In any case, Aristotle taught that the goal of ethics is to find real happiness. This happiness is only found by following the virtues. This doesn't explain where the virtues come from or why they are morally binding on all humans.
>
> And if objective morals are abstract objects, where are they? How did they get there? Why do we feel like we *ought* to behave a certain way, like we've been *commanded* to do a certain thing,

if objective morals are just abstract objects? What would make an object demanding?

It just seems so much more reasonable to assume that we feel like we *ought* to behave a certain way because our feeling of "oughtness" is rooted, or grounded, in God's moral character. Morality feels like an internal commandment because *it is* a commandment. *All humans* experience the Moral Law because God transcends all humans. He's like a rain that makes every human wet.

"But why can't I just be good? Why do you have to bring God into the discussion?"

Well, at this point I'm not talking about being, or acting, good. We're discussing how we can have an objective Moral Law if it's not grounded in an objective moral Being.

"Can they be grounded in the universe?"

No. Remember, nature doesn't tell me how I *ought* to behave. Nature just behaves. If there is a *transcendent* Moral Law, then it must be grounded in something other than Mother Nature.

[Long pause.]

"Do you think that humans perceive of the Moral Law because God designed our brains in such a way that we can perceive them, like antennas can pick up radio signals?"

[Pauses]

The problem with this is that morality, in this case, would be assumed to be composed of matter or energy, which can't be true for morals. The Moral Law is not made of matter or energy, no more than the laws of logic are made of matter or energy. The only explanation I know of that makes the most sense is that our soul has access to God, who is the objective source of morality. That is, objective morals don't exist on their own, as if they are floating around the heavens. Instead, the objective Moral Law, just like the objective laws of logic or mathematics, come directly from the Objective Being, God, who's very character is good.

"So, is it good because God commands it or is it good just because it's good?"

Yes. [Smiles] Objective morals are good because God commands them, and whatever God commands is good because God's very character is good. That is, God is not bound by moral laws, nor are God's moral laws chosen arbitrarily. Rather, moral goods flow from His very nature.

"You think we have a soul? Why?"

Well, I don't mean to beat a dead horse, but I want to make certain you got the point. There is an objective, transcendent Moral Law that all humans know, but do not do all the time. The best causal explanation for the Moral Law is God.

"It's still hard for me to see . . . or admit? . . . that we all follow the same Moral Law."

I never said that we all follow it. I said that we all perceive it. Humans certainly don't follow it all the time!

"Hmm. I'll keep thinking of that one. So, why do you think we have a soul?"

This is the last fact that I mentioned that I believe points to God.

"You think a soul can be proven scientifically?"

I don't think it can be put in a laboratory, but I do think that there is enough evidence from which we can deduce that fact. That is, I think we can work backwards from certain evidences to argue for the existence of the soul.

"What is a soul?"

Philosophers disagree over whether or not animals have souls. If animals have souls, it means that souls have varying capacities. At least for the human, the soul is an immaterial substance that has the capacity of consciousness (it has awareness and can will things), the capacity of reason, possesses a particular personality, and the capacity to apprehend objective moral values. I don't have a problem calling this a "mind."

If materialism is true, then there is no soul because everything is matter and energy. If there is a soul, it means Materialism is false and that the origin of the soul must be supernatural. And the best causal explanation for an immaterial, rational soul cannot be the random, undirected, nonrational processes of nature; it must be from God.

"What evidence do you have for the soul?"

I think there are four things that demonstrate we have a soul: (1) we have consciousness; (2) we have a capacity to reason, (3) we have a capacity to apprehend objective moral values; and (4) we have awareness without a body after death. I'll briefly look at each.

(1) We have consciousness. Roy A. Varghese is certainly correct: "We are conscious, and conscious that we are conscious. No one can deny this without self-contradiction—although some persist in doing so." For example, if you say, "I don't have a consciousness," I'm gonna' respond, "What do you mean, 'I'?" I had a student one time who didn't believe we had a consciousness. I teased him from time to time until one day he said, "You know, the other day I was thinking to myself and I . . .," to which I interrupted, "Wait a minute. To whom were you speaking?" He smiled and said, "OK. You're right."[11]

"Then why do brain studies show that brain neurons are more active when someone's thinking certain things? Doesn't this demonstrate that thinking and consciousness are just neurons firing?"

"First of all, neurons show no resemblance to our conscious life. Second and more important, their physical properties do not in any way give reason to believe that they can or will produce consciousness. Consciousness is correlated with certain regions of the brain, but when the same systems of neurons are present in the brain stem there is no 'production' of consciousness."[12]

And our consciousness gives us the capacity to will things. We have agency. We can decide to do things.

Like I've said before, there is no doubt that our mind and brain interact, but our consciousness or mind is not the brain. Roy A. Varghese says it well: "The point here is that, strictly speaking, your brain does not understand. You understand. Your brain enables you to understand, but not because your thoughts take place in the brain or because 'you' cause certain neurons to fire. . . . [Understanding] is a holistic process that is supraphysical in essence (meaning) and physical in execution (words and neurons). . . . The integration [of the brain and consciousness] is so total that it makes no sense to ask if your acts are physical or supraphysical or even a hybrid of the two. They are acts of a person who is inescapably both embodied and 'ensouled.'"[13]

There is simply no *physical* explanation at all for why we are aware *that* we are aware. That is, there is no materialistic explanation for our being conscious. Our capacity to be conscious must be caused by something that is beyond nature.

(2) In materialism, Reason is the result of an undesigned, high-functioning, evolving brain. Therefore, Reason is nothing more than the natural, undesigned, random result of randomly changing brain matter and chemicals. However, this view is self-refuting. Every thought, including the thought about evolution, cannot be considered "true" because objective truth is illusory. All knowledge becomes mere temporary chemical behaviors in the brain, which is a product of meaningless and random chemical processes existing for survival. This is why Reason cannot be an evolutionary instinct.

Like I said much earlier in our conversation, reasoning is not, as C.S. Lewis reminds us, "a sensation which we feel. Reasoning doesn't 'happen to' us: *we do it.*"[14] Instead, in Christian theism, our soul has the capacity to reason because our souls "do not come from nowhere. Each has come into Nature from Supernature: each has its tap-root in an eternal, self-existence, rational Being, who we call God. Each is an offshoot, or spearhead, or incursion of that Supernatural reality into Nature."[15]

To reiterate one last time, I'm not suggesting that the brain is not related to our ability to reason. While our brain is generated by genetics, our reason is generated by God Himself. "A man's Rational thinking is *just so much* of his share in eternal Reason (i.e., God) as the state of his brain allows to become operative: it represents, so to speak, the bargain stuck or the frontier fixed between Reason and Nature at that particular point."[16]

"You think we only think things because God thinks them *for us?*"

Oh no; thank you for the clarification. I only mean that reasoning is above or beyond natural causes. The *capacity* to reason—not our individual thoughts—must be rooted in God, the objective source of Reason or else our thoughts are just chemicals in our brain moving around and they offer us no truth.

(3) Like we've already talked about, in materialism, there are no objective values, only social constructs or evolutionary-driven survival instincts. This means that there are no objective moral values to apprehend.

However, in Christian theism, we recognize that there are objective values. Our soul, since it exists in the metaphysical realm with God, can perceive of objective moral values.

(4) In materialism, there is no afterlife. As Stephen Hawking once said, "The afterlife is a fairy tale for those who are afraid of the dark."

Fortunately, the "fairy tale" is quite compelling. In *Evidence of the Afterlife*, radiation oncologist, Jeffrey Long, MD, analyzed over one thousand three hundred first-hand narratives and compiled nine proofs from those narratives that our soul exists after our body dies. The following proofs involve the great majority of people who experienced a post-mortem event:

- Lucid death = They were completely aware (with sensations) of their environment while unconscious or clinically dead.
- Out of body = They have no physical constraints and can travel to different parts of the room, building, or world at will. They experience this in "real time" and can recount those events to others when they return. I quote "real time" because they all say that they are aware that something has transpired, but that time is also irrelevant. They say it's as if it's all happening at the same moment, but also that it could have been years.
- Blind can see = People who were blind from birth can see when they are dead. They return telling detailed visual descriptions of their experience (not only colors, but detailed, physical descriptions of objects).
- Impossibly conscious = General anesthesia deliberately causes amnesia and loss of consciousness (among other things). Even though they should be utterly unconscious, when people die, they can have complete awareness during this time, even after prolonged periods of anesthesia.
- Life Review = They have detailed reviews of their lives, reliving all memories *with sensations*. They usually say things like, "I had totally forgotten about that event during my childhood."
- Family reunion = They meet dead relatives (including relatives they have never met, like siblings lost during miscarriages about which they were never told).
- Children agree = Young children tell the same kind of stories (which means they are not borrowing from common cultural images).
- Worldwide consistency = Regardless of race or religion, the stories have several similarities.
- Changed lives = These events radically change their lives (no more fear of death, more loving, etc.). Think about it: very few people wake up from poignant, moving *dreams* and radically change the way they treat people and/or understand their

meaning in life. For those who've died and had experiences, life is forever different.

See how this is much more than the common legend that people just see a "bright white light" and then come back to consciousness?

[Stares at me.]

OK. Here are two examples written by people who have died. These are too incredible not to recount!

This first story starts on a dark note. This woman, Michelle, was shot in the back of the head by her boyfriend while she was attempting to break up with him. The authors continue:

"She left her body, and from a spot in the corner of the room she watched as firefighters and police officers stepped around her body as they tried to figure out exactly what to do. The boyfriend's brother began to cry, and as he did he threw up on a police officer, which was a sight that made her laugh. It was then that she had this revelation about death:

'I felt so blissful and whole . . . full of the most love I had ever experienced. I thought to myself, "If this is dying, then it's not as bad as everyone thinks it is." Then I saw a light from above me. It was pulling me away from the room. I figured it was okay to just let this happen, to go with the flow and accept whatever was to be. The light was getting brighter, engulfing my body. . . . Body? I had no body. It stayed back down in that damp room. I realized that I was dead physically but mentally I was still alive. My soul was now my "body." I looked up into the light. I could see someone beckoning me to come. He was there at the end of this lit tunnel. Then I heard a voice. It was a man's voice. He asked me if I was ready. I felt so good. It was so easy.'"[17]

Or listen to this experience by a little girl:

When Jennifer was eleven years old, she was in a terrible car accident. The authors continue:

"She saw her 'limp and lifeless body' below. The voice of a spiritual being told her she was needed back at the accident site to help the unconscious driver. Here is her experience as she wrote it:

'Then the voice said, "His nose is cut off his face; you will need to go back and help him; he is bleeding to death." I said, "No, let somebody else do it. He will be fine without my help. I do not want to go back down there. No!" The voice said, "I will tell you what to do. You take off his shirt after you pick his nose up off the floorboard of the car. It will be next to your feet and his right foot. Place his nose on his face, pressing down to stop the bleeding. It's just blood, so do not be afraid. I am with you as always." (I knew I was never alone from as far back as I could remember.) "So then, Jennifer, you will begin to walk him up the right side of the road, and a car will come. Tell the man to take you to the nearest hospital. Keep the man calm, and lead him to the hospital where you were born. You know the way and everything will be all right. You must do this. Understand?" Jennifer goes on to say that when she returned to her body everything happened as she was told by the spiritual being. A car stopped and carried them to the hospital where she was born. She was able to calm both the anxious driver and the accident victim who lost his nose. And there was a happy ending: a skin graft was used to reattach the nose with "barely a scratch left to notice." The astonished emergency room doctor said, "I cannot explain what kind of miracle I just witnessed in this emergency room today."'[18]

[Smiles . . . Long Pause.]

"I'm sure there are . . . well, uh . . . responses to all this."

Perhaps. Go read that book I mentioned. The authors deal with all kinds of skeptical reactions. Before I read it, I wasn't sure about any of it. Now I'm completely convinced. There is no remotely possible scientific explanation for any of this. Not now; not ever. It's beyond the natural realm.

[Pause.]

"And even if we do have a personality, or a soul, why can't it be the result of nature?"

That wouldn't make any sense because of the nature of the soul. How could a soul, which is not bound by matter or energy, arise from matter and energy?

"And so you think that God creates souls?"

Yes.

I think it's interesting that the neurophysiologist John Eccles, who won the Nobel Prize in Physiology, says that the evidence forces him "to believe that there is what we might call a supernatural origin of my unique self-conscious mind or my unique selfhood or soul."[19]

The great fifth-century theologian, Augustine, believed that "the soul . . . was made by the all-powerful God."[20] It's not a broken-off piece of God, as if God's nature could change. For Augustine, it was the soul—and he believed that "soul" referred to a creature's capacity to reason—that distinguishes humans from animals. (I think the reasoning is only one of the capacities of the soul.)

He could not decide what the exact source of the human soul is. It was either created by God and placed into the first human, then passed down from the first human to every generation; or is created anew into each human.[21] He concludes that we should either be content with not knowing, or continue in "diligent seeking, humble asking, persistent knocking" in case God reveals the answer to us one day in the future.[22] I'm with Augustine.

"So either the soul is passed down in some soulish way, or God creates each one."

Yeah. Though I tend to think that God makes each soul unique.

"Huh."

Well, to wrap up, in Materialism, we are not conscious, Reason cannot be trusted to discover truth, there are no objective values to apprehend, and there is no explanation whatsoever for any post-mortem experience. In Christian theism, we are conscious, Reason can be trusted to discover truth, objective moral values *do* exist and can be discovered, and there *is* an explanation for post-mortem experiences, all because humans have souls.

"Huh. We've covered a lot of territory."

[Laughing] We sure have! To recap: I think the existence of God is the best causal explanation for (1) the origin of the universe, (2) the origin of multiple, fine-tuned constants throughout the universe, (3) the origin of life, (4) the origin of morality, and (5) the origin of the soul. I believe the most rational belief to hold is that God is the reason there is a universe that is fine-tuned for life, and why there is life, morality, and souls. And as I already said earlier, I'm not suggesting that these things absolutely, conclusively "prove" God exists. Rather, I do think all these things point us in the right direction.

"OK. Fair enough. But this just gets you a deistic god, a distant god that may or may not interfere with the universe."

That's exactly right. It takes more evidence to believe in a particular God. And I think I have that evidence. It comes from Christianity.

But, after all this, are you willing to concede that believing in a Creator God is not some irrational, leap-in-the-dark, fairy tale? Are you willing to concede that a Creator God exists?

CHAPTER EIGHT

Why I believe Jesus was deity

"But you don't just believe in a Creator God, but that your God came to Earth, right? Why should I believe that your God is the only God?"

That's right . . . well, that God the Son came to Earth. I believe in one Creator God as best understood by the life, death, and resurrection of Jesus of Nazareth. And we know primarily of His life from four sources called "Gospels." Now it's important to understand . . .

"But why do we need to believe in a god who interacts with us? Why not just stop with Deism—you know, that there's a Creator God but that God doesn't mess with the universe?"

I don't think we *need* to believe that God interacts with us. If Christianity didn't exist, I'd certainly just be a Deist. Yet, scientific facts certainly fit the truth claims of Christianity. Or, as C.S. Lewis says, "In science we have been reading only the notes to a poem; in Christianity we find the poem itself."[1] Christianity provides a framework for the whole show, not because Christianity provides good scientific methods, but because Christianity gives us the Agent and goal of the universe. In Christianity, science fits perfectly for what we'd *expect to find* as a rational creature observing a rationally-intelligible universe made by a rational God.

"Well, perhaps the universe has some kind of consciousness. Why not just say that?"

Because . . . well, for me, I find no compelling reason to say that. But of course, saying that the universe is "god" is incredibly attractive.

"What do you mean? Why?"

Who wouldn't want to believe in pantheism—that the universe is a kind of energetic battery source? That kind of god doesn't require anything from us. That kind of god isn't a judge. That kind of god isn't moral. As usual, Lewis says it perfectly:

"Speak about beauty, truth and goodness, or about a God who is simply the indwelling principle of these three, speak about a great spiritual force pervading all things, a common mind of which we are all parts, a pool of generalized spirituality to which we can all flow, and you will command friendly interest. But the temperature drops as soon as you mention a God who has purposes and performs particular actions, who does one thing and not another, a concrete, choosing, commanding, prohibiting God with a determinate character. People become embarrassed or angry. Such a conception seems to them primitive and crude and even irreverent."[2]

"Yeah, I see his point. It is easier for me to believe in a god who doesn't do anything or who, at least, doesn't mess with me."

I'm with you . . . if there weren't evidence that God really is personal in the person of Jesus.

"Perhaps . . . well, OK. But how is Jesus' life any different from Mohammed's life? Why don't you believe in him? They were both religious leaders and considered prophets, right?"

Well, that's a big issue, but to be as short as possible, I don't believe Mohammed is God's prophet because I do not find the evidence compelling. And even if we trust everything the Muslims say about Mohammad, he was just a dude. No one would dare argue that Mohammed was Allah incarnate. That is, Mohammed was not Allah-come-to-Earth. Moreover, I find the documents concerning Mohammed, at least in their primary narrative, not trustworthy historically. The life of Mohammed was not written down for a hundred years after his death. There are an overwhelming amount of contradictions, and if you claim that the Quran is directly from the mouth of Allah—as they claim—having contradictions is a *major* problem.

[Looks excited.]

Just in case you're wondering—no, I do not hold the same understanding of God's inspiration of the biblical authors like Muslims have for their book. We can talk later about this if you'd like.

[Looks surprised.]

Also, there are numerous problems with Mohammed's life and theology as it relates to the God of whom Jesus speaks and represents. The idea that the God of the Old Testament would *ever* approve of, not to mention command, killing people *if they did not convert to Judaism*, as is the case within Islam, is absurd! Israel was to be a "light to the nations," not a "sword" to the nations. Perhaps Mohammed's god would do such a thing, but Yahweh (God's name in the Old Testament) certainly wouldn't. Yahweh's commandments to rage war in the Old Testament—the very few times He did—was for judgment on *extremely* corrupt, savage people (e.g., they performed child sacrifice). The same disparity exists between Jesus and Mohammed. In any case, Jesus gave no indication whatsoever that there were other *prophets* coming *after* Him who would *really* fix things. So, the god of Islam acts extremely different from the God of Judaism and Christianity. We're either both wrong or one of us is right in our understanding of God. Again, that's a huge topic that I can't get into now.

"Wait a second! I can't let this slide. Christians claim the same thing about their Bible—that's it's straight from the mouth of God."

That's true for some Christians, but not so for the majority of Christians around the world. I believe that God inspired certain men throughout history to relay what He wanted using their cultural and historical situations. But in any case, and this is crucial to understand,

I did not come to the Bible assuming it's inspired or a divine message. Instead, in my own journey, I assumed the Bible should be examined with the same historical scrutiny as any ancient document: Jewish, Muslim, Christian, Hindu, or whatever. I finally came to the conclusion that God inspired people to write the Bible, but I do not *assume* it. As a skeptic myself, I need any ancient document to stand up to historical scrutiny.

"Isn't the Quran just like the New Testament?"

Unlike the Quran or other ancient texts, the New Testament is *not one* book. It was not *collected* by one person or group. It was not *edited* by one person or group. It is a collection of twenty-seven documents of various literary types, written over a period of around fifty years. The first document is a letter from a man named Saul or Paul (Saul was his Hebrew name; Paul was his Greek name) to a small house church in Thessaloniki, Greece, which is dated to around 50 AD. The last document is probably the document we call the "Apocalypse of John," or Revelation, which is dated probably around the end of the first century. Though there is some wiggle room in the exact years, we know that Jesus lived around 4 BC to AD 33. This means that we have documents that date from within a couple decades of the existence of Jesus. We know that Paul knew of at least one of Jesus' living siblings because Paul mentions in passing that James was Jesus' brother (Galatians 1:19).

Now, we don't have the original documents, since papyrus decays and much of it was destroyed when Christians were attacked, but we have very good, close copies to the originals.

"You don't even have the originals? Why trust them at all? How are you even certain that Jesus even existed. Isn't it much more likely that Jesus never existed?"

There is no serious historian—from atheist to Christian fundamentalist—who believes Jesus didn't exist. There is more mention of Jesus in the ancient sources than for any other historical figure in antiquity.

I guess, for the sake of time, I must say to trust me. This is my field of specialty. No historian denies Jesus existed.

"But what about the original documents? The Bible we have today is based on dozens of translations or something."

No. The New Testament was written in Koine Greek (the Greek spoken and written in the time of Jesus). We have documents written in Koine Greek that date to within a few decades of Jesus' existence. Anyone who studies Greek can read them. All modern translations of the New Testament are based on the Greek.

"All I know is Bart Erhman has written several books about how the Bible can't be trusted, and he has his PhD."

Ever heard of N.T. Wright? Richard Hays? Richard Burridge? Luke Timothy Johnson? Leander Keck? F.F. Bruce? Ben Witherington, III? Larry Hurtado? C.K. Barrett? I. Howard Marshall? Richard Bauckham? Graham Stanton?

"Nope."

I'm not surprised at all . . . but you've heard of Ehrman. He's a real bestseller! These names are a portion of the most preeminent New Testament scholars on the planet, represented at schools across the US and Europe. The reason you haven't heard of them is because they are busy writing trustworthy historical and literary scholarship, not Barnes and Noble sensationalism.

I studied the main monograph by Ehrman, *The Orthodox Corruption of Scripture*, in a PhD seminar on textual criticism (that's the science of how scholars analyze ancient documents in order to get the oldest form of the text). Every other work that you see of his is a watering down of that main work. Bart Erhman is not all wrong; it's just that his overall thesis simply cannot be sustained. His conclusions are only shared by a small minority among New Testament scholars.

His main argument in his works goes like this. We do have around

5,600 copies of manuscripts of the New Testament—*more than any other ancient document by several thousand* (the closest is Homer, for which we only have 643 copies). Yet, we don't have New Testament manuscripts of the gospels before about 220 AD, which is about 150 years *after* the first Gospel was written. That is, the manuscripts we do have might be several generations of copies removed from the originals. So, we don't have the originals. And in the copies we have, we realize that there are numerous mistakes, about 99% of which are simple grammatical mistakes.

So far so good. This isn't controversial; this is universally accepted among textual scholars. But then he continues to argue:

First, since there are so many mistakes in the copies we do have (even though they are almost entirely grammatical), and we must assume that the *earliest* copyists did *worse* because they weren't trained in copying texts, then we have no reason to trust that the New Testament documents are reliable.

Second, scribes changed the text to fit their theological views. Therefore, at best we are forced to be agnostic about the reliability of the New Testament documents. At worst, it could mostly be made up: fabricated to meet the theological views of various groups of Christians across the Roman Empire.

Let me make a few reflective comments.

My first response is that the belief that there was widespread "orthodoxy" among all scribes is patently false. This is why all conspiracy theories fail: it assumes a network of power that simply didn't exist. The people who copied the texts might have had theological agendas (and probably did), but this does not mean that they *all* agreed as to what was "orthodoxy" (i.e., what was perfect Christian theology).

Secondly, Ehrman assumes that the earliest copies we possess are copies of copies of copies (etc.) of the originals. That is, Ehrman assumes that the earliest copies we have today are removed by *countless* generations of copies. But why? There is no reason to assume this. This is pure speculation. The earliest copies we have *could be* the originals! *We have no idea if the manuscripts we possess are the originals (though that's very unlikely) or how many copies they are from the original*. If anything, it's much more likely that we *don't* have countless generations between the original documents and the ones we possess since writing books was both expensive and difficult in the ancient world.

"Where are the copies?"

Mostly in libraries across the US and Europe.

My final reflection concerning Ehrman's work is concerning changes to the texts by the copyists. Were there changes in the copies we have? Absolutely! And we know where they took place and they are no longer in most modern English translations. The average estimate, as attested by the great Bruce Metzger, is that *at least 98% of the original New Testament can be reconstructed with great confidence* (this is far greater than other ancient documents).

"What's an example of something debated or . . . you know . . . different in the manuscripts?"

Here's an example of the kind of "variant" or issue that a textual critic would notice. In Mk 1:41 some manuscripts say that Jesus felt "pity" on a lame person. In some other ancient manuscripts it says that Jesus felt "anger." The "anger" reading is probably the original word, even though most modern translations say "pity" (for various reasons that are way beyond our topic!). Jesus was probably angry. OK. No problem. It's *this* kind of thing that Ehrman's talking about, not whether or not Jesus existed, taught controversial things, died, or was raised from the dead.

"Wow . . . but, in any case, you said that there's a time gap between the Gospel manuscripts we have and the originals. What do you do with that? If there's a time gap, why trust the copies we have at all?"

Nearly every historian and textual critic, no matter *what* their particular religion is, believes that the text we have can be trusted. Why? Because (1) the copies we do have are *so close to the date of* the original events that it's highly improbable that they are grossly distorted or fictional. As the late great textual scholar, Sir Frederic Kenyon said: "The interval then between the data of original composition and the earliest extant evidence become so small to be in fact negligible, and the last foundation for any doubt that the Scripture have come down to us substantially as they were written has now been removed. Both the authenticity and the general integrity of the books of the New Testament may be regarded as finally established."[3]

(2) If there were some scribes who wanted to make up the stories, there is no explanation for why very similar stories about Jesus arose independently in different regions of the Roman Empire. If all the manuscripts came from one town, that might mean there was a conspiracy. But that's not what happened. (3) We have thousands of references to the New Testament in the early church fathers of the second and third centuries which corroborate the manuscript copies we have. If the copies we have were grossly distorted, then why do our copies share so much in common with the early church fathers? (4) The events described in the Gospels fit perfectly with what we know about first-century Palestine and Mediterranean world.

"So, do we have evidence outside of the New Testament about events in the New Testament?"

Oh yes. We have other Jewish, Greek, and Roman literature, along with numerous archaeological finds that corroborate countless facts in the Gospels. It doesn't corroborate all of it, but the corroboration is amazing.

The final reason why scholars think the manuscripts we have are extremely close to the originals is that the textual changes that exist hold no significance. By "significance" I mean that it changes any of the core Christian beliefs.

Scholars know how to spot minor changes and these are all widely known and studied, like the example of Jesus being angry. This is why Ehrman's conclusions are not taken seriously among New Testament scholars.[4] There is absolutely no reason for his alarmist battlecry not to trust the New Testament. In fact, the examples of scribal changes—the ones *he* thinks are earth-shattering—are *insignificant* for any Christian fact or theological view.

"So none of them really matter?"

For example, Greg Boyd, who went to school with Ehrman at Princeton, makes a common critique of Erhman's work:

"Bart's book [*Misquoting Jesus*] makes 'mountains out of mole hills' all over the place. For example, he makes a big deal over the fact that 1 John 5:7, which speaks about the Trinity, wasn't in the original Bible. In fact, it was inserted by Erasmus in the 16th century. But so what? The doctrine of the Trinity has never been based on THAT verse—obviously, since the doctrine of the Trinity was articulated in the first four centuries of church history and this verse wasn't in the Bible these early fathers were using. Not only this, but hardly any scholars have taken I John 5:7 seriously *for the past four hundred years*! That's why it's omitted in all translations of the Bible except the King James Version."[5]

"Wow."

But of course, the wider public is ignorant of these minor variants. This is why these books sell so fast: the general audience thinks this is breaking news! But in fact, there's nothing new about what he's "discovered" at all.

Finally, if we cannot trust the New Testament documents as historically reliable—and don't forget that we have much earlier manuscripts and several thousand more manuscripts than any other ancient text in existence—then we have no reason to trust *any ancient document in the world*. That is, if the New Testament is thrown out, then certainly the rest of ancient literature is eradicated as well.

Go read F.F. Bruce, *The New Testament Documents: Are They Reliable?*, Craig Blomberg, *The Historical Reliability of the Gospels*, or Daniel Wallace, *Revisiting the Corruption of the New Testament*.

Now, if you don't read these texts, it demonstrates that you're only interested in believing that the New Testament can't be trusted. If you're truly open to it, then you'll read both sides. And in this case, Ehrman's conclusions are *overwhelmingly* in the minority among New Testament scholars. (In reality, Ehrman also trusts the manuscripts we have because he makes detailed arguments on specific Greek words *against* traditional authorship by appealing to *other* manuscripts. That is, if none of it can be trusted, or if we must be completely agnostic, how does he make arguments of exact wording from texts he doesn't even trust?[6])

The overwhelming majority of New Testament historians and text critics are convinced the New Testament manuscripts—even though we don't have the originals—can be trusted to accurately reflect the originals. For example, this is what the leading New Testament text critic of the last generation, Bruce Metzger, said about the documents:

"The evidence for our New Testament writings is ever so much greater than the evidence for many writings of classical authors, the authenticity of which no one dreams of questioning. And if the New Testament were a collection of secular writings, their authenticity would generally be regarded as beyond all doubt. . . . From the viewpoint of the historian, the same standards must be applied to both. But we do not quarrel with those who want more evidence for the New Testament than for other writings; firstly, because the universal claims which the New Testament makes upon mankind are so absolute, and the character and works of its chief Figure so unparalleled, that we want to be as sure of its truth as we possibly can; and secondly, because in point of fact there *is* much more evidence for the New Testament than for other ancient writings of comparable date."[7]

"OK. But even if I can trust the manuscripts, what if the Gospels tell stories that are all made up? Why should I trust that the Gospels are telling the truth? Why should I trust that they are historical?"

First of all, I need to make it clear that I do not *assume* that the New Testament can be trusted, either in its manuscripts or in the stories it tells. The New Testament should (and does) hold up to the same scrutiny of any other ancient text. If the New Testament cannot be trusted to be historically true, at least in its broad narrative, then we should not trust it. End of story. There is no reason to assume fairy tales are historical. There should be no cheap passes. No matter how much a person might *want* the story of Jesus to be true, it doesn't make the narrative of the New Testament historically reliable.

"Well, I agree."

The first thing scholars do to determine if an ancient narrative is considered historical is to attempt to classify the literature's type, or genre. Determining genre is crucial. You and I do it all the time, instinctively. It probably doesn't ever cross your mind when you read a newspaper that you have just picked a particular type of literature that is very distinct from a fictional novel or a cookbook. In fact, if you were to read the newspaper like you did a cookbook, you would radically misinterpret the newspaper. If you were to read a John Grisham novel like you did the newspaper, you'd radically misinterpret the novel. Literary type matters. We need to know the type so that we interpret it correctly.

So it is with ancient literature. Scholars try to figure out what the author intended his genre to be. This is especially easy, at first glance, if the author actually tells us what kind of literature he intends to write.

Well, the consensus among New Testament scholars for the last several decades is that the Gospels are different kinds of ancient biographies. You can go read Richard Burridge, *What are the Gospels?: A Comparison with Graeco-Roman Biography*, to get all the details. In any case, the fact that they are forms of ancient biographies means that the authors most certainly were not writing fictional legends. In fact, in the gospel of Luke, the author tells us that he is intending on writing a "diegesis," or "orderly account or narrative," which in ancient rhetoric, is a particular type of historical biography.

The ancient biography is like modern biographies in a few ways, the most important of which is the fact that biographies are chiefly about one main character, not about tons of political events (like a social studies textbook might be). However, in the ancient world, the authors didn't care that much for details about the main character, such as his physical attributes, what he ate, the names of his dogs, and all of his daily patterns.

"Right, like of Winston Churchill."

Right. You might expect such details in a biography about Winston Churchill—not so, for the most part, in ancient biographies. Instead, ancient authors were much more concerned with crafting a story that brought out the way the author *interpreted the main character*. If the author wanted to make certain the audience understood how caring the main character was, the author would make certain that there were plenty of stories in the narrative that demonstrated that point, and so on. Anecdotal stories might be fictional, but on the whole, authors of biographies attempted to recount stories as they had received them from first-hand experience or from eyewitnesses. And no matter what, the stories in the biography attempted to emphasize the character of the main protagonist.

This doesn't mean that everything in an ancient biography can immediately be trusted to be historically true, or that the authors could not embellish or be creative in their narratives (in fact, certainly they did to various degrees, since that was encouraged in the ancient world), it just means that there is no historical basis for dismissing the narratives as utterly or primarily fictional.

In any case, I don't need to argue for the historical proof of every single fact of the New Testament. All that really matters for me is to determine if Jesus existed, what his chief message was, and if he really died and rose from the dead. Since there is no reason whatsoever to dismiss the Gospels as historically unreliable, if you'd like, we can discuss what Jesus said about himself.

"But why should I trust the Gospels, since they're written by converted people? I mean . . . they're obviously biased. They're certainly not objective."

You're absolutely right. They were biased. They were converted. That's right. Can you help me understand why this means we shouldn't trust the documents?

"Because they're not objective. They're just spiritual propaganda."

But the myth of an *objective* author, or historian, is fiction. So, are you saying that you dismiss every single first-hand account of the Holocaust because Jews are clearly biased? If the Jews who experienced the Holocaust don't count, then where do we get our history from? The Nazis? They can't count either since they are not objective. Germans? Not them, because they were there too. We're left with archaeological remains, I guess. How do we fit the archaeological pieces back together to reconstruct history if we can't use any literary or oral evidence?

"Well, I don't know."

The authors of the Gospels were not objective. Historians don't care about their objectivity; they care about whether or not the facts in their stories are objectively true (i.e., did they really happen as described). So, the question that matters is, Can we determine if they were telling the truth? Or, one might ask, "Why did they convert? What caused them to write these documents?" It's like asking, "Why did the Holocaust survivor write the book about surviving the Holocaust?" Of course the author is biased—extremely biased, we'd suspect!—but the *events* she recounts can be examined apart from her particular bias.

"I hear Christians talk all the time about Jesus being God. But, I can't find anywhere in the New Testament where Jesus says, 'I am God.' Besides, if Jesus were God, then who did Jesus pray to?"

These are good points. Can I start with the second question? I certainly confess that Christians are often unaware of the confusion their vocabulary can bring. When Christians say that Jesus is God, they mean that Jesus is deity, not that Jesus is God *the Father*. God the Father, God the Son, and God the Spirit are three distinct persons, or centers of consciousness, which *together* are one Being, whom we call God. They all share the same essence or "deityness." We can chat about Trinity later if you're interested. In any case, orthodox Christianity is adamant on this point: Jesus is not God the Father. So, when Jesus is praying, He is praying to God the Father—a different center of consciousness—not to Himself.

Now, concerning your first question, the short answer is, "you're right." There is no place where Jesus says, "I am God." The early Christians sure spoke that way about Jesus after Jesus' death and resurrection, but Jesus apparently never did speak about Himself in that precise way.[8]

But of course He didn't. When the Bible says, "God," it is almost always a shorthand way of referring to God *the Father*. Therefore, to claim "I am God" would have been interpreted by every Jew in the audience to mean that Jesus thought He was God *the Father*. Jesus didn't think He was God the Father, nor did He want His audience to think that.

"So why do you think that Jesus was deity if He never claimed to be?"

This can only be answered by situating Jesus within a first-century Jewish context. I know this sounds really strange to us in this day and age, but Jews thought that time as we know it will come to an end because God will stop it. And when they speculated on the end times, they believed that God would send an emissary to do His work of ushering in the close of this age. This figure would get people's hearts and minds prepared for God's judgment. This figure would attempt to help people restore the broken relationship they had with God.

This figure is what they called a "Messiah." Jesus clearly thought *He was this anticipated Messiah* (Mk 14:61-62). But more than that, Jesus thought that he was best understood as a modified version of the Messianic figure, the "Son of Man," who is found in the biblical book of Daniel, chapter 7. We need to talk about this figure.

All New Testament historians concur on this point: Jesus

understood his role as the "Son of Man." It appears 83 times in the Gospels (e.g., Mk 2:1-12; 8:31; 14:60-64). "Son of Man" in most passages of the Bible can simply mean, "person." Yet, when Jesus says it, He is referencing a particular figure in the writing of Daniel. Who is this figure? What does he do?

In Daniel 7:1-14, we meet the "Son of Man." He "comes with the clouds of heaven" (= in the Divine presence), where He is presented before the "Ancient of Days" (= God the Father) and given full authority to rule over every single person and nation on the Earth. Every single person and nation will serve Him, and His reign and kingdom will never end or be destroyed.

Jesus assumes that He is the Son of Man figure. That is, Jesus assumes that *He shares the divine prerogative to be God the Father's emissary and rule over all creatures on Earth.* Jesus assumes throughout the Gospels that if they do not want a loving relationship with Him, they do not want a loving relationship with God the Father. If people do have a loving relationship with Him, then they have a loving relationship with God the Father.

"Wow. That's pretty bold."

Now, to a Semitic thinker (which all Jews were and most still are), God is primarily understood in a functional way. If it quacks like a duck, walks like a duck, and so on, then it must be a duck. They wouldn't dissect the duck and detect its chemical composition before declaring it was a duck. That is, function was the chief way to determine what something was. They didn't focus much at all on something's "essence."

So, the question is: what did an ancient Jew think that God (or deity) *did*? Only deity *creates, judges, gives commandments, and forgives; and is worshipped and prayed to.*[9] So, to determine if Jesus was deity is to determine if Jesus did things that only deity can do. It's an implicit way of thinking about it, rather than looking for Jesus saying, "Hey buddy, I'm God."

What's so interesting is that all these functions of deity appear in Jesus' life and in the early church's claims about Jesus.

"Really?"

Yep. Jesus created things, such as bread and fish (Mk 6:38-44; Jn 2:7-10; 1 Cor 8:6; Col 1:16; Heb 1:2). The Hebrew word for "create" that's used in the Old Testament is only used for God because only God brings something into existence that wasn't there before. Jesus did the same thing. Moses did not create. Mohammed did not create.

Jesus judged and will judge all moral creatures (Matt 7:21-23; 11:20-24; 19:28-30; Lk 18:8; Jn 5:30; 8:16). Not only did Jesus judge and believe He will judge at the end of time, but that He had the authority to say that his disciples will judge *alongside* him under His authority (Matt 19:28; cf. 1 Cor 6:2; Rev. 20:4)! Moses will not judge humanity on his own authority, nor could he have given that privilege to other humans. Mohammed will not judge humanity on his own authority, nor could he have given that privilege to other humans.

Jesus gave commandments (Matt 28:18-19; Jn 8:51; 13:34). Think about it: no Jewish teacher would have dared act like he had the authority to offer new, binding commandments on all humans! Jesus did. What would people think of you if you went around telling people that they have a new commandment to follow, no matter what their race, gender, or economic status was? Moses didn't give commandments to all humans based on his own authority. The same is true of Mohammed.

Jesus forgave people for sins they committed against Himself *and for sins they committed against other people* (Mk 2:5-11; 9:2; Lk 7:48; Jn 5:22; Acts 2:38; 5:31). I cannot overemphasize this point: in Jesus' time, every Jew believed that *only* God the Father offered forgiveness (e.g., Mk 2:7) and this forgiveness was offered *only* through the sacrificial system at the Temple. Jesus assumed that *He* could forgive sins and that He could do it apart from any need for sacrifice whatsoever. And Jesus didn't just forgive sins done against Him. He told people that *the sins they had committed to others* was forgiven. Ever done that before? Ever walked up to a total stranger and said, "I forgive you." Moses didn't forgive sins. Mohammed didn't forgive sins.

Jesus was and is worshipped (Matt 14:33; 28:9; Lk 24:52; Jn 9:38; Phil 2:3-8; 1 Tim 6:15-16; Rev 5:14). Again, it's one thing to pay homage to a king; it's another thing to worship someone as if you are in the presence of deity. No one worshipped Moses. No one worshipped Mohammed.

Jesus was and is prayed to (Jn 14:13-14; 15:7; 1 Cor. 1:2; cf. 1 Thess 3:10-11). Now this last one is more controversial in New Testament studies because evidence that *Jesus* encouraged people to pray to Him comes from the Gospel of John. John has a really precarious place in historical studies. It's unclear if during Jesus' own lifetime He required or encouraged people to pray to him. Nevertheless, early Christians sure did it. Do you think Jews ever pray to Moses? Abraham? Do you think Muslims pray to Mohammed? Of course not. These figures are all dead, and no one thinks they are deity, which means they can't answer prayers. But at least in the Gospel of John, Jesus encourages it. And if you don't trust the author of John, then you can trust Paul's letters to demonstrate the fact that early Christians did pray to Him because they assumed He was deity.

And on top of all this, the early Christians acted just like Jesus was deity *from the earliest evidence we have.*

As Larry Hurtado, who has written the most comprehensive look at early devotion to Jesus, makes clear: "[T]here is an implicit but astonishingly close association of Jesus with God, both in the attributes and functions they share in earliest Christian beliefs (e.g., Jesus as the agent of creation, dispenser of the Holy Spirit, and eschatological judge) and in the reverence accorded to both in early Christian devotional practice."[10]

"No. I read this book that said that Jesus was considered a man until the Council of Nicaea in 325. That's where he was declared to be a god."

Well, this is a PhD in Historical Theology talking, but that's patently false. No such thing was "declared" or decided at that council. Go read John Behr, *The Nicene Faith*, or R.P.C. Hanson, *The Search for the Christian Doctrine of God.* I also encourage you to read the ancient sources yourself and see if you can find a shred of evidence for that common legend. Everyone at the council of Nicaea assumed Jesus was deity. They were debating, amongst other things, exactly *how to talk about Jesus' deity* in relation to God the Father.

No, from the very first year of Christianity, apparently all primitive Christians believed Jesus was deity.[11] In fact, by the time of the letters of John (within a few decades of Jesus) there were people claiming that Jesus only appeared human! John has to write letters encouraging his people not to give in to such lies: Jesus clearly came "in the flesh" (1 John 4:2-3), and to say otherwise is patently false.

"But isn't it true, at least, that early Jews thought Jesus was just a man, but that Paul founded Christianity?"

The evidence doesn't support that conclusion. Larry Hurtado concludes emphatically: "[The] evidence confirms how astonishingly early and quickly an impressive devotion to Jesus appeared. This in turn helps explain why and how it all seems to have been so conventionalized and uncontroversial already by the time of the Pauline mission to the Gentiles in the 50s."[12] Later he says again that "a veritable explosion of devotion to Jesus took place so early, and was so widespread by the time of his Gentile mission, that in the main christological beliefs and devotional practices that he advocated, Paul was not an innovator but a transmitters of tradition."[13] That is, Paul did not create Christianity.

"How do you know the earliest Jews believed Jesus was deity?"

There are many evidences to demonstrate that the primitive Christians believed Jesus was deity. For example, there is evidence in the fact that songs were written to Jesus as if He were deity. These come from the very first year(s) of the church's existence (e.g., Phil 2:5-11). This is unique among Jews. No Jew would dare write songs— for worship services!—to a regular dude.

In a similar vein, the apostle Paul could intertwine the foundation of Jewish theology (called "the Shema") with belief in Jesus. The Shema is a very important text in the Old Testament, and it's said regularly by Jews to this day. It states that there is only one God and that we should love that one God with all our heart, soul, and strength (Deut 6:4-5). There's a great example of Paul joining this crucial monotheistic creed of Judaism with belief in Jesus.

At one point in Paul's letters, Paul recognizes that Greeks think that their religious statues (or idols) actually represent real gods. But Paul responds in opposition: "Yet for us there is one God, the Father, from whom are all things and for whom we exist (= like the Shema), and one Lord, Jesus Christ, through whom are all things and through whom we exist" (1 Cor 8:6). In a first-century Jewish context, this is a truly amazing statement!

Not long after he wrote that statement, Paul said a similar thing in Colossians 1:16-17: "For by him all things were created, in heaven and on earth, visible and invisible, whether thrones or dominions or rulers or authorities—all things were created through him and for him. And he is before all things, and in him all things hold together." To equate God the Father's creative, sustaining power with Jesus' creative, sustaining power is unheard of in any type of Judaism that has ever existed. And we have no record that the other primitive Christians were outraged when Paul said this. It's just assumed he's right: the appropriate thing to do is to equate God the Father's role with Jesus' role.

It's also seen in the fact that everyone is healed and baptized "in Jesus' name" (e.g., 1 Cor. 6:11; Acts 2:38; 4:30). No Jew was baptized in Moses' name or healed in Abraham's name. That would be nonsense at best; blasphemy at worse. It was apparently a commonly-held view of the earliest Christians that believing in the risen Jesus could heal you and that He gave you a new life of forgiveness in baptism. And this is not centuries down the road with tons of theological reflection; this is in the most primitive evidence we have.

Another aspect of primitive Christianity is the fact that all early Christians believed Jesus was the living *Lord*. "Lord" meant ruler or master. No Jew would have ever thought of a dead man as their *present, living Lord*. The primitive Jewish Christians believed that Jesus was made Lord at his resurrection. For example, Peter's speech to the Jewish leaders at Jerusalem says, "Let all the house of Israel therefore know for certain that *God has made him* both Lord and Messiah, this Jesus whom you crucified" (Acts 2:36). This is assumed

throughout the New Testament. You can't turn a page without seeing it. For example, Paul can say that "when you are assembled in
the name of the Lord Jesus and my spirit is present, with the power
of our Lord Jesus" (1 Cor 5:4) they are to discipline a certain immoral
person in their congergation. It's just assumed that the risen Jesus'
power is present with them *because He's the living Lord.* The primitive Christians even wrote a song which declares that at the name
of Jesus "every tongue [will] confess that Jesus Christ is Lord, to the
glory of God the Father" (Phil 2:11). This is a radical political statement
in Roman society, where the average person commonly declared,
"Caesar is Lord."

I cannot be more emphatic on this point: no Jew would have possibly "called upon" the name of Jesus in prayer and worship unless
they thought Jesus was alive and well in the Heavenly realm with
God the Father, able to actually *do something*; that is, to listen to
their praise, or answer their prayer request. No Jew would have ever
"called upon" the name of Moses or Abraham. Those men were
dead, ancient Jews believed, alive only in a shadowy existence, and
most certainly *not* ruling over the cosmos as "Lord." Jesus *is* "Lord."
He *is* King.

It's also implicit in the way the primitive Christians conceived of
Jesus: He was perfectly moral. It is consistently asserted that Jesus
never committed one sin (implicit in the Gospels; 1 Pet 1:19; 2:22; 1 Jn
3:5; 2 Cor 5:21; 4:15). Who does that?

One reason that Muslims revere Mohammed is because it is said
that he repented more than seventy times a day.[14] That's a whole
lot of sinning! Of course, if you came and lived in my house for three
years (that's the amount of time we think that Jesus' ministry lasted),
I can *guarantee* that you would *not* be telling the world about how
sinless I was. I can't imagine being around someone who never ever
said something inappropriate, not given into temptation, or wasn't
selfish at least once!

"Hmm."

Notice how I haven't talked about Jesus healing or performing miracles: other people throughout history have supposedly done that. If they did or didn't is irrelevant; it doesn't make a person deity to perform miracles. But, it is worth noting that Jesus did, in fact, perform around thirty-five miracles in the Gospels. This is surely more than any other ancient figure. Even Jesus' opponents admitted that Jesus performed miracles (they just claimed that such power came from an evil source).

Then of course, there are references scattered throughout the New Testament that speak of the fact that the earliest Christians thought Jesus was deity. For example, Thomas declared to Jesus: "My Lord and my God!" (Jn 20:28). John says "the Word (= Jesus) was God" and "the Word became flesh" (Jn 1:1, 14). Paul says that Christ is "God over all" (Rom 9:5) and "in Christ all the fullness of the Deity lives in bodily form" (Col 2:9). The author of 2 Peter declares that believers receive righteousness from "our God and Savior Jesus Christ" (2 Pet 1:1). Matthew believes that Jesus is "God with us" (Matt 1:23). The author of Hebrews says that "the Son is the radiance of God's glory and the exact representation of His being, sustaining all things by His powerful word" (Heb 1:3).

Ever hear this kind of talk about Mohammed? Moses? Joseph Smith? Confucius?

"But couldn't you say that the reason why early Christians thought Jesus was a god is because so many Greek people came in the church? They didn't have a problem believing that a god came to Earth since they believed many of their gods had come to Earth."

Well, it's highly unlikely that the Greeks *actually* believed their gods came to Earth. We have every reason to believe that even the ancient Greeks understood the distinction between legend and history.

Concerning Christianity, remember, the earliest *Jewish*-Christians *already* believed Jesus was deity. It was not a belief that came with the Greeks later the in history of the church. Hurtado says it well again: "[D]evotion to Jesus as divine erupted suddenly and quickly, not gradually and late, among first-century circles of followers. More specifically, the origins lie in Jewish Christian circles of the earliest years. Only a certain wishful thinking continues to attribute the reverence of Jesus as divine decisively to the influence of pagan religion and the influx of Gentile converts, characterizing it as developing late and incrementally. Furthermore, devotion to Jesus as the 'Lord,' to whom cultic reverence and total obedience were the appropriate response, was widespread, not confined or attributable to particular circles, such as 'Hellenists' or Gentile Christians of a supposed Syrian 'Christ cult.'"[15]

"OK . . . but, I have no problem saying that Jesus was a moral teacher. I follow the teachings of many great people, such as Confucius, the Buddha, Mahavira and Moses."

Considering the fact that Jesus believed He forgave sins, and that He was the Son of Man figure spoken about in Daniel who had all of God the Father's authority to rule over creation, I can't see why anyone would want to call this guy a "great moral teacher." I really don't.

There is a well-known quote by C.S. Lewis that makes this point. It's worth repeating:

"Among these Jews there suddenly turns up a man who goes about talking as if He was God. He claims to forgive sins. He says He has always existed. He says He is coming to judge the world at the end of time. Now let us get this clear. Among Pantheists, like the Indians, anyone might say that he was a part of God, or one with God: there would be nothing very odd about it. But this man, since He was a Jew, could not mean that kind of God. God, in their language, meant the Being outside the world Who had made it and was infinitely different from anything else. And when you have grasped that, you will see that what this man said was, quite simply, the most shocking thing that has ever been uttered by human lips."[16]

"Well, he might have said some good things . . . like the Sermon on the Mount."

Have you read the Sermon of the Mount before? It's some of the most demanding sayings of Jesus we have recorded.

"Yeah, but he says some good things."

Sure. I concur. I just mean, why take to heart anything Jesus says at all if this guy thinks He can forgive sins and rule over creation? He sounds like a lunatic!

I could go down to the local insane asylum, steal some journals from some of the people in there and discover some real "nuggets of truth" in their writings. Would you call these mentally insane people, "great moral teachers" because you found some "nuggets of truth"? Would you start following anything they said?

[Smiling] "Maybe."

[Laughing] OK. Well, this is another place where you and I differ.

I just don't see a way around it: Jesus was either absolutely crazy; thought He was right, but was wrong; was lying; or was right. If he's crazy, mistaken, or lying, then why in the world should we listen to *anything* He has to say?

"How are you so certain he was right?"

The resurrection. If it didn't happen, in my opinion, then Jesus' teachings should barely be considered. But the resurrection did happen. He was telling the truth.

What gets me is: *most* people who met Jesus in His ministry didn't think He was crazy, mistaken, or lying.[17] Some did think he was driven by evil.[18] But in general, the response He got the most was awe.

Again, I love how C.S. Lewis says it:

"[Jesus made] claims which, if not true, are those of a megalomaniac, compared with whom Hitler was the most sane and humble of men. There is no halfway house and there is no parallel in other religions. If you had gone to Buddha and asked him, 'Are you the son of Bramah?' he would have said, 'My son, you are still in the vale of illusion.' If you had gone to Socrates and asked, 'Are you Zeus?' he would have laughed at you. If you had gone to Mohammed and asked, 'Are you Allah?' he would first have rent his clothes and then cut your head off. If you had asked Confucius, 'Are you Heaven?' I think he would probably have replied, 'Remarks which are not in accordance with nature are in bad taste.' The idea of a great moral teacher saying what Christ said is out of the question. In my opinion, the only person who can say that sort of thing is either God or a complete lunatic suffering from that form of delusion which undermines the whole mind of man. . . ."

"We may note in passing that He was never regarded as a mere moral teacher. He did not produce that effect on any of the people who actually met Him. He produced mainly three effects-Hatred-Terror-Adoration. There was no trace of people expressing mild approval."[19]

In my opinion, what Jesus said and did should be utterly dismissed or utterly embraced. If you join the compelling historical evidence of the Gospels with the resurrection, there is every reason to embrace what Jesus said and did as true. As the former atheist, J. Budziszewski, has said: "If the Christian revelation about Jesus Christ is true, then it makes no sense to do anything else except to follow him."[20]

[Long pause.]

"Hmm . . . So, you said that if the resurrection didn't happen, then you wouldn't trust Jesus was telling the truth. What do you mean, 'resurrection' and how do you know it really happened?"

CHAPTER NINE

Why I believe Jesus was resurrected

Do you know what the word "resurrection" means?

"When someone comes back to life, right?"

Yes and no. If a person comes back to life immediately in his or her previous body, then that's called "resuscitation." That's not what "resurrection" means. The primitive Jewish Christians did *not* claim that Jesus was resuscitated. They claimed that Jesus was resurrected.

And to know what primitive Christians meant by that term, we need to talk a little bit about what Jews in the first century meant by "resurrection." Now, before I begin, you need to know that the definitive work on the resurrection is from N.T. Wright, *The Resurrection of the Son of God*. Its seven hundred pages will keep you busy for a while! He researched Jewish, Greek, and Roman literature from before and after the time of Jesus. His work has been very helpful to me and I'll deliberately use him in our discussion.

Here are a few important facts about resurrection as understood in the ancient world. First, Greeks and Romans believed death was the end. While there were individual legends of gods reappearing after death as ghosts or in dreams, pagans didn't believe that humans would come back to earthly life after they died. Death was a one-way street and there was no turning back. After closely examining all of the Greco-Roman ancient literature, N.T. Wright concludes:

"We cannot stress too strongly that from Homer onwards the language of 'resurrection' was not used to denote 'life after death' in general, or any of the phenomena supposed to occur within such a life. The great majority of the ancients believed in life after death; many of them developed . . . complex and fascinating beliefs about it and practices in relation to it; but, other than within Judaism and Christianity, they did not believe in resurrection. 'Resurrection' denoted a new embodied life which follow whatever 'life after death' there might be. 'Resurrection' was, by definition, not the existence into which someone might (or might not) go immediately upon death; it was not a disembodied 'heavenly' life; it was a further stage, out beyond all that. It was not a redescription or redefinition of death. It was death's reversal."[1]

So, no Greeks or Romans believed in resurrection.

Second, only a few groups within Judaism believed in resurrection (like the Pharisees).[2]

Third, Jews that did believe in a resurrection believed resurrection to mean that *after one dies, at some time in the future, God would reanimate one's former body to live on Earth.* At no time in the literature does "resurrection" mean a spiritual existence (though it could refer metaphorically to Israel being rescued from exile). Resurrection of a body always and only meant corporeal, or physical, or bodily, life.

Fourth, they also believed the resurrection to be a corporate event. That is, when it happened, it happened either to every human, where they all went to judgment, or it only happened to the righteous faithful. Either way, no one individual would be raised.

Fifth, the resurrection would only occur at the end of time. When you saw the dead reanimated, it was the sign that the new world-to-come as promised in the prophets had begun.

Finally, the Jews that did believe in a resurrection didn't make a "big deal" of it; it was an issue not discussed often.

"So what does this have to do with Christianity?"

Well, the earliest Jewish Christians shared some of these ideas in common, but also held to key differences. That is, when the earliest witnesses claimed to have seen Jesus in a resurrected body, they didn't describe it in the same way as other Jewish contemporaries were describing it. There were similarities, but also important differences.

For example, instead of resurrection being a peripheral issue, early Jewish Christians made the belief in resurrection *the central belief.*

Paul says that if the resurrection didn't happen then a Christian's faith is futile (1 Cor 15:14). Everything in the Christian faith rests on the resurrection actually happening. It must be an historical fact or the whole religion is false. This is a huge difference from every other Jewish writing we have before, during, and after the New Testament.

Second, instead of the resurrection only occurring at judgment, Jewish Christians divided the resurrection into two halves: Jesus first and others later. This is another huge difference.

Third, because the resurrection only happens at the end of time, Jewish Christians believed that the end of time had already begun because of the resurrection of Jesus.

Finally, because of their experience with Jesus, they discovered that the resurrection was *not* just a resuscitation of a corpse, but *a transformation of an old body into a new, incorruptible body* that works in the World-to-Come.

"Why does it matter that early Christians changed things from what others were saying?"

It implies that they didn't simply draw from common beliefs and make up stories. Think about it: it means that *independent sources* (Matthew, Mark, Luke, John, and Paul) describe the resurrection of Jesus in similar ways to one another; yet all of them are *dis*similar from what other Jews were saying was "supposed" to happen in a resurrection. This makes the stories much more historically reliable!

If I interviewed five people *independently* (like the four Gospels and Paul), and they all gave similar accounts about an event *in ways that were unlike what anyone else had ever said*, I would certainly be convinced that they were telling the truth. If their stories were exactly the same, I'd assume collusion—that they'd gotten together and agreed that they'd tell a certain story. Yet, if there were differences in the details, but similarity in their main points, I'd believe it.

Moreover, if the Gospel writers were making up a story, it is much more likely that they would have widely divergent stories, and that they would have plagiarized Old Testament descriptions of the resurrected dead. But this is not what we find. Their stories are all the same on the main points, and none of them just hijack some Old Testament stories and make up a new version.

"Oh, so you're saying that if they were to make up stories, they'd just borrow stories from their Jewish writings or whatever?"

Yes, that's right. As N.T. Wright says, "Nothing in Jewish literature or imagination had prepared people for a portrait like this. If the gospel writers had made something up to fit a preconceived notion, the one thing they would certainly have done is describe the risen Jesus shining like a star (according to Dan. 12:3), [since] this was how the righteous would appear at the resurrection. But Jesus didn't. His body seems to have been transformed in a way for which there was neither precedent nor prophecy, and of which there remains no second example."[3]

"Where is your evidence for the resurrection? I mean, historically? You know we can't trust the Bible for all of your evidence. They were biased."

Wait a second. Every document written in the history of the world is written by someone who's biased. Remember, we talked about this concerning World War II and the Holocaust.

"Oh yeah. But, . . . but they're not talking about miracles."

Oh, again we're back to Materialism. Materialism is false, i.e., there is more to existence than matter and energy. Since God exists, miracles are certainly possible.

But, . . . I tell you what. Let's do this. Let's forget the miracle-aspect of the stories. What do virtually all New Testament scholars agree upon? What can we know for (almost) certain? (1) Jesus' tomb was found empty by women after He was buried in it by Joseph of Arimathea; (2) the earliest witnesses believed Jesus had appeared to them in bodily form; and (3) disciples and certain enemies of Jesus abandoned many cherished beliefs and practices of their former lifestyles and gave total devotion to Jesus because they said He was the

Messiah and living Lord. I believe that the resurrection is the best explanation for these facts.

"Again, where do read about Jesus' resurrection?"

We learn about the resurrection from five sources: the early letters of Paul, especially 1 Corinthians 15, which is based on oral tradition that dates to the first few years if not months of the resurrection; and the Gospels: Matthew, Mark, Luke, and John, which contain primitive material as well. These are five independent sources. Having this many independent sources is unparalleled in the ancient world.

"OK. Even if we admit Paul's account, which is early, why should I trust the Gospels, which were written later?"

This is crucial to understand. Historians of ancient stories are not interested in the date of the *writing*. They are interested in the date of the *oral tradition* that the writing contains. The ancient world was an oral world. Over ninety percent of people in the Roman world couldn't read or write. They possessed powerful memories. So, what matters the most is the dating of the oral tradition that is contained in the written material.

This reminds me of a documentary I was watching the other day concerning the American Prohibition, which outlawed drinking alcohol. There was a woman interviewed who gave detailed descriptions of certain "speakeasies" she visited . . . *ninety years earlier*. The amount of detail she recalled was fascinating, and she's not even from an oral culture!

One could argue: "But her testimony is irrelevant! That interview was conducted ninety years after it happened!" But wouldn't you think this is nonsense? Shouldn't her interview count as historical *even though it was documented ninety years after the fact*?

And with 1 Corinthians 15 and the Gospels, we're not ninety years removed, but barely two decades removed. And this *written* record is based on an *oral* tradition that goes back to the very first years, if not months, of the resurrection!

Now, if you accept Paul's testimony, then we have enough. Among scholars, Paul's account is considered the most primitive evidence for the resurrection. Here's what Paul says: "For I delivered to you as of first importance what I also received: that Christ died for our sins in accordance with the Scriptures, that he was buried, that he was raised on the third day in accordance with the Scriptures, and that he appeared to Cephas, then to the twelve. Then he appeared to more than five hundred brothers at one time, most of whom are still alive, though some have fallen asleep. Then he appeared to James, then to all the apostles. Last of all, as to one untimely born, he appeared also to me (1 Cor 15:3-8)." If you accept that, then this is enough. This is incredibly primitive material.

"But what about the Gospels? Can they be trusted?"

N.T. Wright argues that there are four reasons why we should trust the historical accuracy of the Gospel narratives.[4]

First, like I said, if an ancient Jew wanted to fabricate details about something, they would typically use their Bible, the Old Testament. We know this as historians because when Jewish authors do it, they heavily allude to and quote Old Testament texts. Interestingly, this is what we *do not* find in the resurrection narrative. The resurrection narratives are almost entirely void of scriptural references. If you argue that scriptural references were originally in the Gospels, but were *taken out years later*, then you'd have to believe that each author did it *independently*. This scenario is extremely unlikely and there is no evidence of this.

Second, in ancient Jewish culture, women were not considered reputable witnesses. In fact, when Paul speaks of the tradition of the resurrection in 1 Corinthians 15, he never mentions women. Most scholars agree that by the time of Paul's written record (mid-50s), the women have been omitted from the story because their inclusion was embarrassing. Yet, the Gospels are very clear on this point: women were the very first witnesses to the resurrected Jesus. It is highly improbable that this is fictional.

Third, like we said before, the stories of Jesus' body are unheard of in ancient Jewish or Greco-Roman literature. If they were fictional, we should expect tales that describe Jesus as a shining star (from Daniel 12:3) or like a ghost. This is not what we find. Instead, Jesus' body is physical. Jesus' body can be grasped and he can eat. Yet, He is also able to appear in rooms suddenly.

Finally, we know that the early Christian communities, when reflecting on the resurrection, interpreted and applied what they thought the resurrection meant *for them*. That is, they reflected on the significance and application of the resurrection to their lives. They did this, overall, by emphasizing (1) baptism (we "die" in the water and rise to new life when we come out) and (2) the future hope that *all* the faithful will be resurrected like Jesus. However, what we do not find at all in the Gospel narratives are these two important reflections. There is no mention of baptism or of future hope. This fact makes sense if the narratives are primitive. If the Gospel narratives were late, we would expect to see Christian theological reflection smuggled in, but we don't.

"But what about the differences that are in the Gospels?"

There are differences in the Gospels. There are. It's unclear how many women went to the tomb; it's unclear if the disciples met Jesus in Jerusalem or Galilee first; etc. And we should expect minor differences to be if they are independent and based on such radical news. If the narratives were all the same, we'd assume that there was collusion or only one tradition. Instead, we have several different traditions that point to the same basic narrative.

"But why are these just 'minor'?"

Because those differences don't change the central story. The Gospels and Paul agree on the fundamentals: Jesus was crucified under the charge of sedition (i.e., claiming to be King), buried by Joseph of Arimathea, his tomb was found empty by women, and Jesus appeared to some of his disciples and to enemies.

"But it could have been any number of things that caused them to make up these stories."

Right. I concur. It is easy to make up alternative stories: they were delusional; they were liars; they wanted to die. But stories don't convince me; evidence does. There is no alternate story that's ever been offered that explains all the data. And even if you join several hypothetical stories together, you only multiply problems because there is no evidence for any alternate story you offer.

"But isn't it much more likely that the Christians made this up because they wanted power?"

What possible power could they have received? They were the minority. Additionally, they were persecuted on and off for centuries. They had no possible power to gain.

"Perhaps they had a great religious experience. They really missed Jesus and made up these stories to make themselves feel better."

OK, but why call Jesus the Messiah? There is no way that any Jew would have claimed that a crucified "criminal" was the conquering Messiah and Lord expected among Jews. By the way, there were a few "Messiahs" before and after Jesus. N.T. Wright says it well: "When Simeon ben Kosiba was killed by the Romans in AD 135, nobody went around afterward saying he really was the Messiah after all, however much they had wanted to believe that he had been."[5] If a disciple would have said, "We've seen Jesus." Their friends would have said, "We miss him too." No one would have possibly added, "And He's the Messiah."

And don't forget Paul. Remember that he, in his own words, "persecuted the church of God violently and tried to destroy it" (Galatians 1:13). Even if Jesus' disciples had a religious or emotional experience because they missed Jesus, this can't possibly explain why an enemy of the Church converted to Christianity. No; the only reason a leading opponent of the Church would abandon hating Christians to becoming one of them is if he met the risen Jesus Himself. And that's exactly what happened. Paul met the risen Jesus. It changed his life.

"How do you know Jesus really died? Perhaps he wasn't really dead. You know that Muslims say that Jesus never died."

Romans had been crucifying people for centuries. They knew how to do it. And even if they didn't, are we to believe that a whipped, beaten person survived bleeding in a cave for three days? Even if he did, why didn't anyone mention how he was still wounded? Why claim that Jesus had been *risen from the dead* (Matt 28:7; Acts 3:15; cf. Mk 9:9; 2 Tim 2:8), rather than risen from a rough night of beating? How can he appear in rooms suddenly? How can he disappear from their sight?

"What if they saw a ghost?"

Jews believed in ghosts. At one point in Jesus' ministry the disciples thought they saw a ghost on the Sea of Galilee (which turned out to be Jesus walking on the water; Mk 6:49). Greeks and Romans believed in them. Yet, no one thinks the risen Jesus is a ghost. If Jesus were a ghost, then how could someone hold him (John 20:17, 27)? How could Jesus eat (Lk 24:42-43)? Why say that Jesus had been resurrected, when resurrection *always* meant a physical body? "The best explanation by far for the rise of Christianity is that Jesus really did reappear, not as a battered, bleeding survivor, not as a ghost (the stories are very clear about that), but as a living, bodily human being."[6]

"But they wanted him to be raised from the dead."

[Laughs] No they didn't! I'm not laughing at you; I'm laughing at how ironic your statement is in light of the evidence. The disciples could not have been more obtuse on this point. Not one single person was expecting this, which is really odd if Jesus did, in fact, tell them repeatedly that he would be resurrected (Mk 8:31; 9:31; 10:33-34). He has to convince people (e.g., John 20:25-27). It would seem that the common sentiment among the disciples was that they had put their hope in a failed Messiah. As one disciple said it, "We *had hoped* that he was the one to redeem Israel!" (Luke 24:21). The disciples were convinced that they had backed the wrong horse. No one saw this coming. Not one single disciple, from the evidence we have, was longing and hoping that Jesus might rise from the dead. Ancient Jews expected what we *still* expect, for dead people to stay dead.

"What if someone just stole the body?"

Why? What could be their motive? . . . Perhaps they could steal the body to bury it in a grave of their choice. But there is no evidence for this at all. Moreover, there is no indication in any Christian document that exists that Jesus' tomb was ever venerated. You can go today to Jerusalem and visit the venerated tombs of dead rabbis from two thousand years ago. It was the custom of the deceased family to visit the tomb, especially on the anniversary of the person's death, and have a meal at the tomb. Nothing of the sort was ever done at the tomb of Jesus.

Moreover, the Gospels record that the tomb was protected by Roman guards. Even if there were no guards, why would the disciples go around telling people that Jesus had been raised from the dead, that He was the Messiah, the living Lord, and get persecuted and (for some of them) killed for something *they knew was a lie*? And how do you explain the fact that Jesus appeared to Paul?

[Stares off in the distance.]

Let me put it to you this way. Here are the facts about which almost every historian of primitive Christianity would concur: Jesus really existed and was crucified around AD 30. (1) All of his disciples abandoned Jesus by not dying beside him on a cross; (2) The remaining disciples in Jerusalem remain in hiding for fear of being killed because of their association with Jesus (none of them have any desire to become martyrs); and (3) they all believe Jesus was *not* the Messiah because of his death. (Remember: Jews were convinced that Messiahs cannot suffer and die!)

Then, *something* must have happened.

Because within a few months of Jesus' death, the disciples and thousands of other Jews, including some Pharisees and priests (those who *opposed* Jesus during His life) make radical changes. (1) They make Sunday the chief day of worship. (2) They begin baptizing people *in the name of Jesus*, only once (though they had always baptized themselves multiple times in their religion). (3) They begin healing and forgiving people in the name of Jesus. (4) They begin "eating Jesus' flesh" and "drinking Jesus' blood" in a commemorative meal that celebrated a new covenant between God and humans (even though no Jew would have ever invented a story that made them sound like cannibals!). (5) They begin writing new songs that honored Jesus as Lord and God. (6) They begin praying to Jesus, assuming that He was the living Lord. Finally, (7) they begin suffering persecution and for some, death, for their proclamation of a risen Jesus.[7]

So, here's my question: *what happened*?

What possibly could have happened that would explain *all* of these radical changes for a huge group of people— people who once utterly opposed Jesus as a false prophet during his lifetime?

[Smiles.]

If you're a Materialist, that is, if you're convinced that miracles cannot happen because there is no God, then none of this will compel you. You will make up *any story you can* and call it "more historically probable."

And I would agree . . . that is, if I were a Materialist. When Materialists say that an alternative theory is "more historically probable," they *really* mean, "it's an explanation that better fits my predetermined materialistic worldview." But Materialism is false. Moreover, none of their alternative theories answers *all* of the historical facts sufficiently.

Instead, when I analyze all these facts together, I'm forced to say that the most probable causal explanation for these radical changes among the Jews is the physical resurrection of Jesus of Nazareth.

N.T. Wright, after a lifetime of research on the topic concurs: "And the historical argument is quite clear. To repeat: far and away the best explanation for why Christianity began after Jesus's violent death is that he really was bodily alive again three days later, in a transformed body."[8]

[Long pause.]

And I'm trying to be clear here: I don't believe in the resurrection *because* I'm a Christian. I'm a Christian *because I believe the resurrection appearances are historical facts*. That is, when I analyze the data as objectively as I possibly can, I believe that the physical resurrection of Jesus is by far the best causal explanation for the rise of Christianity.

So, I then work backwards and concern myself with what He taught and did. Why? I ask myself, Why would God the Father resurrect a delusional or lying lunatic? He wouldn't. Like I said a second ago, the resurrection means that everything Jesus said and did was true and that Jesus really is the Messiah. It means we should have a lifestyle that is modeled on Jesus. "If Jesus has been raised, that means that God's new world, God's kingdom, has indeed arrived; and that means we have a job to do. The world must hear what the God of Israel, the creator God, has achieved through his Messiah."[9]

This is the main thing. No matter what challenge comes to Christianity, this is the foundation. Disprove the resurrection and you've disproven Christianity.

"Huh . . . Well, I've never thought about Jesus' resurrection in the light of ancient Judaism. I always just assumed that the earliest Christians were Greeks or whatever and had no problem believing in man-gods. If they were all Jews, then that religious context changes things."

That's right.

[Long pause.]

And when I study what Jesus *said and did*, I'm struck with a phenomenal figure. What I find so compelling and attractive about Jesus is not the titles He uses for Himself or the titles others give to Him. Instead, it's what He taught, it's His demeanor, it's His character, it's his how He treated people.

According to Jesus, everything He taught and did demonstrated His main message: the reign of God. See, that's the reason humans were created: to live under the reign of God, where humans love God with their whole selves and their neighbors like they love themselves. This is what it means to live under God's reign.

God had originally wanted humans to live in this kind of love relationship with God and others, but they kept destroying the love, peace, and fellowship God intended. So, God made covenants with Jews—"OK, Jews. Let's try it this way. I'll make a covenant with you. It'll be like we're married. I'll be your God and you'll be my people and we'll experience the loving relationship I intended. Now, I'll focus just on you, but my intention is that once you live out the *lifestyle of love* that I desire, the entire human race will be drawn to me. Then, the whole human race will join you in a love relationship with me. Deal?"

But, as history demonstrates, they couldn't keep the deal. God sent prophet after prophet attempting to get them back on track. But they didn't listen well enough. It's like a coach at a soccer game, screaming out directions. "No, run that way . . . there you go, now kick the ball . . . nope, not that way, this way . . . right . . . yes! You did it! Now pass it to that guy . . . no, not that way." Finally, the man who *created the game of soccer* decides to do something radical—something he had ever done in the history of the game. He put on a jersey and walked onto the field. "Look. Here. Follow me. Let me show you how to play perfectly the game I designed."

Jesus "walked onto the field" for us. He showed us what a perfect covenant-keeper would look like. He showed us what the reign of God looks like. And what exactly does that look like? Jesus was constantly hanging out with people that no one else would: drunkards, prostitutes, and those enemies of the Jews—tax collectors.

It's amazing how kind, gentle, and forgiving He was to people. At the same time, He was adamantly opposed to false religiosity, those who pretended to be self-righteous. He condemned hypocrites and defended the poor and sick. He exorcised demons and healed people. He extended forgiveness over and over again, even to those who brutally beat and crucified him! This lets me know that wherever God is fully ruling or reigning, the "last shall be first" and the humble, poor, and broken are fully accepted and forgiven through Jesus. Jesus' ministry still captivates me. The fact that Jesus did all of this for you and me is overwhelming.

[Long pause.]

I haven't talked much up to this point about the death of Jesus because our discussion's been more about history than theology. But it's important that I mention, at least a little bit, that Jesus (and the early Christians) believed that His own death *actually did something for those who become His disciples*. The New Testament gives several metaphors for what happened on the cross, but the fact remains: Jesus' death enabled me to have a reconciled relationship with God the Father.

[Looks confused.]

We can talk more about it later if you'd like. It's just that I can't speak about what Jesus said and did, along with his resurrection, and not mention the fact that Jesus' death was saving for me. And look ... I know ... if Jesus were just a "dude," then His death has nothing to do with me. Since Jesus wasn't just a "dude," humans can actually participate in Jesus' death. Jesus bore the punishment for our breaking the covenant with God upon Himself.

"We needed to be punished? What did I do?"

When someone does something immoral, like steal, murder, or whatever, don't you feel like that person should be punished?

"Well, yeah, I guess."

Me too. We call this "justice." This sense of justice comes from God. And God's justice is infinite; He is the source of justice. You and I deserve to be punished because we've all broken God's Moral Law repeatedly throughout our lives. We've demonstrated that we have, in fact, not loved our neighbor as much as we love ourselves, nor have we loved God with our whole selves.

"Yeah, but I've never murdered anyone. I'm no Hitler."

Me neither. And when you and I compare ourselves to the worst example we can think of, we'll always feel pretty righteous. It's like arguing that I'm a great artist by comparing my drawings to my four-year-old daughter. We shouldn't compare ourselves to the worst person, but to the best. Remember, Jesus showed us what a perfect citizen of the reign of God looks like. When we compare ourselves to Jesus, we don't look so nice and well-deserving. We look like sorry wretches.

"But I can never be that perfect. Neither can you."

I concur! We can't. This is why we must be given a gift, a favor, a handout by God. And this favor is given through Jesus' death. In Jesus' death, the Judge took the punishment of our immorality—all of the evil behavior that we've ever done—upon Himself. It's like we owed God a great, unrepayable debt, and Jesus' paid it for us.

As N.T. Wright says well: "The death of Jesus of Nazareth as the king of the Jews, the bearer of Israel's destiny, the fulfillment of God's promises to his people of old, is either the most stupid, senseless waste and misunderstanding the world has ever seen, or it is the fulcrum around which world history turns. Christianity is based on the belief that it was and is the latter."[10] This certainly means that Jesus' death is not some trivial byproduct of the vicious Romans, but the chief way humans should understand the love of God. He didn't have to die for us, but He did. "The cross is the surest, truest and deepest window on the very heart and character of the living and loving God; the more we learn about the cross, in all its historical and theological dimensions, the more we discover about the one in whose image we are made, and hence about our own vocation to be the crossbearing people, the people in whose lives and service the living God is made known."[11]

"Are you telling me that God's forgiveness is a gift?"

Yes I am. Imagine having a disease that guaranteed a violent death. When you see the doctor and receive the news of your diagnosis, you begin to freak out. It really sinks in how sick you really are. Then the doctor looks at you with a smile: "You know what? I was diagnosed with the exact same illness. And there are thousands of so-called cures that get you nowhere. But there's good news: there's one pill that actually cures the illness." Would you shout back at the doctor, "How dare you?! In a world full of medicines, you really think that *your* medicine is the *only* medicine that works? How close-minded of you!"

[Laughs] "Probably not."

Me neither. I'd take the medicine.

[Nods]

CHAPTER TEN

Why I believe I've met the Spirit of the risen Jesus

"Well, I'll think about that death stuff later, I guess. But you said a long time ago, if I remember, that you think you've had religious experiences that corroborated, or confirmed, Christianity?"

That's right. We can think of it this way. One of the easiest ways to know a starving person has found food is by seeing the effect that eating has on the person. The person's body will begin to fill out. The person's skin color will begin to look healthy again. In the same way, one of the easiest ways to know if someone that you've never met in person exists is to see if that person has had an effect on other people. Do other people speak as if they've met this person? Does their face light up or frown? Do they tell stories of interactions, funny anecdotes, or traumatic experiences?

Of course, these experiences need to be corroborated by others. If a woman acts as if she has a best friend, but no one else has experienced her, then the woman might have an imaginary friend. However, if billions of people have experienced the same friend, then it's more likely that the friend exists.

I know I've talked a lot about scientific facts that I believe point to the existence of God, why I have every reason to trust that the resurrection occurred, and why I think Jesus really is the Messiah.

But all this so far has been pretty cerebral. It's like giving you tons of facts about my wife. The problem is, I don't love facts. I love a person. The same is true with Jesus. I love *Him*, not facts about Him.

And I know this will sound like I'm delusional if you don't believe in God, but I believe I've encountered God in a personal way. Of course, I couldn't see Him or touch Him, but I still think I've encountered

God to some degree and at various times. And there are billions of people around the world, throughout history, who have had similar experiences.

"Right. People from other religions also speak of religious experience."

Not nearly as much as you might think. Also, they might speak of mystical experiences, such as enlightenment, but I'm not talking about that.

"Huh."

Let me ask you this: what if someone could communicate *without* physical limitations? What if someone's thoughts could just be *directly* transmitted into your mind?

"So, imagine having a conversation without needing to hear or see something from someone else. Isn't this what delusional people do?"

Well, yes, kind of, except their "conversational partners" can't be corroborated to exist.

"Why does this matter?"

You've just described what Christians believe happens all the time by God's Spirit. We believe that God speaks to us on the inside. Very few of us have ever, in the history of Judaism or Christianity, heard an audible voice by God. The Bible makes it clear that when that happens, the person is never confused about God's message!

Instead, He *introduces thoughts into our minds.* God is not limited by physics. He doesn't need to make an audible voice for our eardrums.

"So why doesn't every Christian hear the same thing all the time?"

For the same reason my children don't hear the same message every time I speak to them. God is a living Being, not a broken record echoing through space.

"I mean, why don't more people hear from God like you do?"

First of all, to be clear, I'm not trying to imply that Christians have constant "marching orders" from God. I'm not suggesting that Christians are little antennas who receive orders from God so we'll know what to drink, eat, and how to drive our cars. We have the Bible. The Bible is our chief source of knowledge for what God wants in the world. Whatever Jesus cared about, we care about too. What the Bible condemns (e.g., greed, dishonesty, gossip, apathy toward the poor) or supports (e.g., loving your neighbor, sacrifice, or service), we do the same. If a Christian thinks that God has given some special revelation to her or him, it is a very big deal, and it must jive perfectly with what the Bible says.

"How do you know if you've got His message right?"

Like I was saying, the message will fit into the character of God as revealed through Jesus in the Bible. This is exactly why we are instructed as Christians to "test the spirits" to see if it flows from the character of God.[1]

"Oh."

Another way of thinking about "hearing" God is that He affects our intuition; i.e., there are times we feel an intuitive sense of things. This often feels like morality. It feels like that sense of "I know I ought to do X." Often times, God's "voice" feels just like that moral, intuitive compulsion or peace. In fact, this is why I typically call God's "voice" a "*peaceful compulsion.*"

Yet, God's voice is not the same as moral intuition. I'm here referring to those times when God gives us a sense that we ought to make a decision that is not explicitly moral.

For example, I'm convinced that God led me or gave me a strong, peaceful compulsive sense of whom to marry and where to go to graduate school (along with several other major decisions in my life). Neither of these are explicitly moral: it would not have been immoral to stay single; it would not have been immoral to marry someone else; it would not have been immoral to go to a different school than the one I chose. Nevertheless, I felt a strong sense of "oughtness" in these decisions, as if I were making a moral decision. I credit this to the Spirit of God.

And perhaps now you can see why this experience is difficult to describe. Christians are really required to use metaphors when talking about "hearing" God. We don't really mean "hearing" God, as if we can hear an audible noise, but we mean hearing Him on the inside.

"Does this happen all the time?"

Well, it's not all the time; and it shouldn't be. Like I said, the chief way that Christians know what God wants is by reading the Bible. But, when religious experiences happen, they're peaceful, joyful, and fulfilling. This is what we mean by a "religious experience." It can involve burning bushes or bright lights or fantastic dreams, but for most Christians, it's not that dramatic.

"And these experiences have helped you?"

Absolutely. In fact, in the past, when I doubted Christianity the most, I simply couldn't get past those daggum experiences. I would absolutely swear by them. That is, when my moods were against Christianity, and I was most ready to reject my faith, I couldn't dismiss those religious experiences.

There have been some really big events that I can think of. I remember when I first became a Christian. I think I was six. My Pastor at my church came over to bring thirteen various kinds of snakes. And he said that if I got bit by more than five of the snakes, I'm not ready for Jesus.

[Stares in horror.]

[Laughs] Just kidding! My pastor did come over to my house one night and joined with my parents and me to pray to God. I was interested in trusting in Jesus, so we talked and prayed. I had a strong sensation of peace and love, and God made it clear to me that He loved me. This is really difficult to describe. Adults who became Christians later in life are usually able to describe this better than those of us who became Christians early in life. That night changed my life.

Growing up, I always really enjoyed science, especially anything having to do with space. During middle school and high school, my mind was made up that I was going to be an astronaut. I took all the Physics classes I could. I even won an award in an Aerospace class. I was told by someone that 99% of astronauts had served in the military and that the Navy Air Guard was the best, so I spoke with a Navy recruiter. (Though I know the Air Force might disagree!)

During the spring semester of my senior year in high school, I had a total change of mind and heart. I had always been active in church, but during my senior year, I devoured several Christian books and workbooks. I developed this profound desire to be at church all the time, and it had nothing to do with a girl! It's weird: it was as if I was starving for God and I couldn't get satiated. All of my work in Physics and Aerospace classes, and anything else I had done to prepare for space, no longer held my attention. I had no outside explanation. I had not joined a cult, drank some special Kool-Aid, or had a near-death experience. Nevertheless, a real substantial change was taking place in me.

One night, when I had returned from a church Bible study at First Baptist Church of Nashville, TN, God called me to full-time ministry. I was listening a cassette (does that tell you how old I am?) of an artist named Wayne Watson. And right there, in my mom's car, God told me on the inside that my insatiable desire for Him was put there by Him. I remember, with tears coming down my cheek, that I would give my entire life for His work if He wanted me to. He basically said, "That's exactly what I want." I've never looked back.

I still enjoy science; I still get a sense of awe when I learn anything new from cosmologists. But, I'm as certain that God called me to be a minister and teacher for Him as I am certain that I exist. It is fundamental to my identity. I couldn't possibly imagine doing anything else. That night changed my life. I went from dreaming of commanding a space shuttle to teaching and preaching at churches. It's like having a radical change in palate.

I remember when I had my initial visit to Gardner-Webb University, where I received my first two degrees. I had a strong, peaceful compulsion inside me that said to attend that school. I had no doubt in my mind: God was calling me to go there. While there, I would meet my wife.

I could give several other major, life-changing religious experiences. Minor events happen often. The minor ones take place all the time while reading the Bible and praying.

"So, how you do know you're not delusional?"

Of course, I could have been delusional. But I'm convinced I'm not.

In the movie, *The Book of Eli*, Denzel Washington's character, Eli, is telling a young woman why he is on a divine mission to return a book to the west coast. He tells her of this internal voice that told him to take the book and how he will be protected because a path will be made for him. The woman makes a crazy face and says, "You did all that because a voice in your head told you to?" I can really relate to Eli's reply: "Yes . . . I know what I heard. . . I know what I hear. . . And I'm not crazy." I know what love feels like; I know what emotional moments feel like. I am quite sane and cerebral. I have no disorders.

I've had emotional experiences listening to music, grieving at a funeral, watching a movie, playing with my children, or during therapy with a counselor. I've *never once* left a highly emotional experience and said, "I've encountered someone tonight."

What makes religious experience so different from every other purely emotional experience I have had–and some I've had were *very emotional and cathartic*–was the sense that *I was affected*. That is, I encountered something *other*, or rather, *someone* other.

These were not like any other event in my life. My emotions were involved, so it was subjective in that sense. But, every time I have these experiences, I feel *as if I'm in someone's presence.* Ever feel someone's presence in the room even though you hadn't seen them yet?

[Smiles.]

I've never once seen the wind, but I feel its presence nearly every week of my life.

And often times, I leave these experiences with a sense of purpose and direction: *as if someone had told me what to do.*

So, to recap: (1) these experiences were so emotionally and psychologically powerful; (2) I felt as if I was affected by something *outside myself;* (3) the experience left me with some lifestyle charge or direction that aligns perfectly with the Jesus we meet in the Gospels, and (4) I've met countless other people who also attest to these kinds of experiences.

I know these are facts. I am certain that they happened. They are as true and as real, and in many respects more real, than any other experience I've had. Nothing anyone will ever say will convince me that I did not experience what I've experienced. You'd have just as good of chance convincing me that I've never met my wife or that I never went to school for my PhD.

So, when I put *all* these facts together—the experiences, the sense of personal presence and direction, the correlation between what I experience and what I know in Christianity, and the corroborating testimony from countless Christians—*based on what I do know*, I infer something: I *believe* I've had experiences with the Spirit of Jesus.

Of course, in the end, I can't completely explain my experiences. It reminds me of the final scene in the movie *Contact*. Ellie, the atheist scientist, after having received information from an alien race, takes a journey to the alien's planet. Unfortunately, when she comes back, she has no scientific proof of her journey. After the congressional committee has drilled her with questions concerning this alleged journey experience, they finally demand proof. She admits she can't provide proof and the audience gasps. With tears in her eyes, she recounts her experience:

"I had . . . an experience. I can't prove it. I can't even explain it. All I can tell you is that everything I know as a human being, everything I am, tells me that it was real . . . I was given something wonderful. Something that changed me . . . A vision . . . that tells us we belong to something greater than ourselves . . . that we're not—that none of us—is alone . . . I wish I could share it. I wish everyone, if only for a moment, could feel that sense of awe, and humility . . . and hope. That continues to be my wish."[2]

Ditto.

[Stares off]

CHAPTER ELEVEN

Odds and ends

"Well, I know it's getting late. But even if all this is true, I still have some questions."

I bet! We've just scratched the surface on countless issues. But, before we're done, what are some of the big questions you still have?

"For example, why doesn't your God answer prayer more? Why don't we see miracles all the time like apparently Jews and Christians used to? And . . . the Trinity just sounds so ridiculous to me. I just don't see how it's not contradictory. Oh, and what about evil and suffering? If your God is so good, why is their evil? And what about all those evil things your God does in the Bible? And don't you believe that people go to hell if they don't think like you do? What about hell? What about the billions who don't agree with you or who never hear about Jesus? And . . ."

These are great questions! Let's tackle one at a time. We'll just briefly talk about some of these, if that's OK, since we'll be here forever if we don't! I'll also try to recommend books to read that will say much more than I will.

Though, I do want to point out first that none of your questions disprove God or any of the truth claims of Christianity. What I mean is, if Christianity is true, then these issues bear no threat to anything we've talked about so far. But, I do want to give more of an answer than that.

"What do you mean?"

I mean that it seems incredibly common among skeptics to assume that if there is a peripheral issue that they don't like, it disproves God. For example, perhaps you don't like the fact that evil exists.

[Shakes head.]

I don't either. But this is no way means God doesn't exist. In my experience, these issues you raised are treated like the main "thing" and they're not. *If it's not about the resurrection, then it's not the main thing.*

"OK. But I would like for these things to make sense."

First, let's chat about prayer. Prayer throughout the history of Judaism and Christianity has never been merely about asking God to do things for you. It involves much more than that. "Communion" might be a good synonym, not "begging."

Secondly, God does answer prayer requests. That is, from those of us on the "inside" of faith, it seems clear that God can, and does— though not always—answer prayer requests. But, we don't expect God to answer every request. God is not a cosmic Santa Claus who grants us our wishes. He is a living Being who actually wills certain things. If I don't answer my child's request, does that mean I cease to exist?

"Well, no."

So, the *amount* of answers to requests is irrelevant. Now, I certainly confess that, in my opinion, Christians often give credit to God for things for which they have no good reason. It is highly probable that many of the "answers to prayer" concerning people's recovery from illnesses are just natural results of a phenomenal human body.

"But what proof do you have for answered prayer?"

There is no scientific proof for answers to prayer. That is, I cannot prove a *causal* relation between my request and the event I believe is the answer. C.S. Lewis gives a perfect example of what happens. One day Lewis had intended on getting a haircut before traveling to London, but he discovered that he no longer needed to go to London. So, he decided to not get a haircut. Nevertheless, "there began the most unaccountable little nagging in my mind, almost like a voice saying, 'Get it cut all the same. Go and get it cut.'" So he did as the voice commanded. The barber there was a Christian, and when Lewis entered the door, the barber said, "Oh, I was praying you might come today." Lewis says that had he come a day or so later he would have been no help to the barber.[1]

This kind of thing happens to Christians all the time. It happens to me often. I will feel like someone is telling me in my mind to call a friend to check on him and when I do call, the person needed encouragement. I will feel burdened to pray for a person who later tells me that she or he had been going through a rough time.

Again, there is no way to prove this in a laboratory. And even if we can prove complete success in having every request answered, it would not prove that God answers prayer. "It would prove something much more like magic—a power in certain human beings to control, or compel, the course of nature."[2]

"But why pray if you don't get what you want?"

Because I don't pray to get what I want. I pray to get what God wants. Jesus taught us that the chief request in prayers is "not my will but Yours." Surrendering is the Christian's fundamental demeanor.

"But wouldn't it be really good of God to answer every request? Like for cancer patients or starving people?"

Perhaps.

"Perhaps! Come on, you don't think . . ."

No, really, perhaps. As a human, I have very limited perspective. I am painfully aware that I do not see how even my small acts are putting things into motion that will one day affect someone on the other side of the planet. Of course, it seems in the short time that curing that cancer is a good. But perhaps that person's survival on this Earth will not accomplish what God wants in the long term. We can't be short-sighted in what we ask God for.

"God wants people to die?!"

Well, hold on a second. My son might consider me evil for not immediately answering his request to get off the doctor's table once the first shot causes him pain. I refuse to answer his request to relieve him of his circumstance and pain. Why? Because I know that the remaining shots he's about to experience make him immune to illnesses that can kill him. I have a perspective my son does not.

But I'm certainly not suggesting I have a constant, deep-seated peace waiting on God's answers or that I enjoy not having my requests answered. On my good days, I accept His will. But there are plenty of times when I'm quite impatient. I certainly wish I could fully understand why certain prayers are left unanswered. I often times wish God *wasn't* working through humans. I like quick fixes like anyone else. Nevertheless, this is where I'm thrust back to the prayer Jesus prayed: "not my will but Yours." Lewis' reflection is helpful:

"He could, if He chose, repair our bodies miraculously without food; or give us food without the aid of farmers, bakers, and butchers; or knowledge without aid of learned men; or convert the heathen without missionaries. Instead, He allows soils and weather and animals and the muscles, minds, and wills of men to cooperate in the execution of HIs will. . . For He seems to do nothing of Himself which He can possibly delegate to His creatures. He commands us to do slowly and blunderingly what He could do perfectly and in the twinkling of any eye. He allows us to neglect what He would have us do, or to fail. Perhaps we do not fully realize the problem, so to call it, of enabling finite free wills to co-exist with Omnipotence. . . This is how (no light matter) God makes something—indeed, makes gods—out of nothing."[3]

We can't forget that God's intent from the very beginning was to use humans on Earth, not to intervene every time suffering occurred. N.T. Wright is right on: "God has committed himself, ever since creation, to working *through* his creatures—in particular, through his image-bearing human beings—but they have all let him down."[4] To say it again: God wants *to use* humans in the reign of God. We are participants in what He is doing. And no matter how impatient I get with God, I have the privilege of trusting in a loving God who has earned my trust, even when He works through us faulty humans.

"If God loves us so much, why isn't everyone happy and healthy?"

It's crucial to understand that God's chief concern for humans is *not* our happiness and physical health. Jesus' proclamation of the reign of God made this perfectly clear. Humans exist to love God, be loved by God, and love our neighbor as we love ourselves. Jesus never once taught us that we'd all be much happier and wealthier and physically safe if we'll just do certain things.

"So then why does God allow evil if He's perfectly good?"

It's important to make a distinction here. Evil is what humans do when they choose an immoral act. That is, evil is a moral act, a corruption of the good, and only humans are bound by the Moral Law. Suffering is when a creature, human or otherwise, suffers pain. So, a person can experience suffering when other humans do something evil or when something occurs in nature that causes pain.

Like everything we've discussed, this is a huge topic! So, please keep reading about this issue if you're not satisfied (e.g., C.S. Lewis, *The Problem of Pain*, or Alvin Plantiga, *God and the Problem of Evil*). Let me make several reflections if that's OK.

First, nothing can take away the feeling that pain hurts. Intellectual answers do not ever solve the need to grieve. Intellectual answers can give us proper perspective, but they don't make us think that evil and suffering are good things. It's the emotional impact of evil and suffering that keep most people from God. We don't like it. I concur. I don't either. But this has nothing to do with God's existence or the truth claims of Christianity.

At least in Christianity, I know that God cares for our suffering and inspires humans to be His hands and feet to a hurting world. In Buddhism, suffering's not actually real, it's an illusion. In Daoism evil and suffering is just a cosmic force opposed to *yang*. My point is, Christianity makes the most sense out of evil: it's a corruption of the good. God hates evil and we do too. Jesus' death, remember, was in response to evil in the world.

Second, ancient Jews and Christians never saw suffering or evil as evidence that God didn't exist. This is a modern problem. They might question God's goodness for a short time but they never abandoned belief in His existence or the covenants they had with Him.

Third, why is suffering and evil only a problem when *other* people cause suffering and evil? Why aren't we outraged about the suffering and evil we cause? Have you ever ceased to believe in your *own* existence or goodness when you choose something immoral or cause suffering?

"Well, no."

Me neither.

Fourth, it is crucial to remember that "good" in Christianity does *not* mean "that which causes pleasure and minimizes pain." Good means "that which conforms to the Moral Law as grounded in God's very character." This makes it clear that I can be in immense pain and God can still be good.

Again, I would argue this is the most difficult challenge for non-Christians. At bottom, we're convinced that if God were good, he'd make certain that we'd never suffer intense pain. But that's a feeling. Intellectually, this is not compelling at all.

"But why is there suffering and evil in the first place?"

Nearly all suffering in the world is caused because God created free moral agents who choose evil. Humans have the freedom to choose both moral and immoral actions. God is not to blame for our evil actions. Genocide, murder, greed, gossip, rape, theft, and all evils are caused by humans. At the same time, charity, love, forgiveness, reconciliation, and all types of moral goods can be caused by humans. It is the risk God takes in creating free agents.

"But what about natural disasters? Why all that suffering?"

I don't know why God designed the world the way He did. He didn't ask my opinion on how to do it!

But for example, look at earthquakes. Hugh Ross reminds us that "without earthquakes or plate tectonic activity, nutrients that are essential for life on land would erode off of the continents and accumulate in the oceans. After a while, life would be impossible on land, though you'd still have life in the oceans. Thanks to earthquake activity, that stuff in the oceans gets recycled into new continents. We see here on Earth precisely the right number and intensity of earthquakes to maintain that recycling, but not to such a degree that it's impossible for us to live in cities."[5] (And isn't it astonishing how people who live along fault lines can get so mad at God for the destruction caused by an earthquake?)

Hurricanes also serve numerous functions in the climate of the planet. Hurricanes are "nature's safety valve—a means for the fluid systems of the planet (such as air) to redistribute the excess heat energy received in tropical latitudes, transporting it toward the cooler poles."[6] Moreover, hurricanes redistribute nutrients that help numerous types of species.[7] The same hurricanes that kill humans help the planet stay healthy. (Isn't it astonishing how people who live among common routes of hurricanes can get so mad at God for the destruction caused by a hurricane?)

The same rain water that gives drink to billions can drown us. The same gravity that allows us to build entire civilizations and cultivate the land also causes deaths when people fall off cliffs. The point is, if we only point out the destruction nature does *to us*, we have again, missed the big perspective.

And we must remember that in countries with the most suffering, Christianity is thriving the most. In countries with less suffering, such as Europe and parts of the US, Christianity is diminishing.

"God could not have designed a planet where we didn't need hurricanes and earthquakes?"

I guess. But as a Christian, I assume that the design of the planet allows the perfect environment in which to allow free-willed humans to love God and each other. Like I said earlier, these free-willed humans are *supposed to love* their neighbors as much as they love themselves. If we did, we could alleviate most suffering on the planet.

"What are you talking about?"

If humans acted like God wanted, there would be no starvation. There would barely be any suffering concerning illnesses. Think how many diseases would be cured by now if we spent the amount of money on finding cures as we do on entertainment. More than 1.2 billion people live on $1/day.[8] And Americans spent $433 billion dollars in 2010 on entertainment and media, compared to global spending at $1.4 trillion.[9] 1.4 trillion dollars on *entertainment and media* in one year! If we increased our giving $19 billion between now and 2015, humans would eradicate malnutrition and starvation; increase it another $12 billion over the same four years, and we'd provide education for every child; increase it another $15 billion and we could provide universal access to clean water and sanitation.[10] We *discard* enough food in the US to feed all of the poor we have.

This is not God's fault: it's completely ours. Humans are to blame for why millions are dying every day in suffering.

It's a whole lot easier to get mad at God than it is to get mad at our own race, no matter how misdirected our anger is.

"Still, are you also telling me that it could be in God's will that people die?"

Remember, for Materialists death is the ultimate end. Therefore, life's chief goal is survival. While some atheists have no fear of death, for most, it seems, death is to be avoided at all costs. But for the Christian, physical death is not the end. Because of Jesus' resurrection, bodily death is stage one of our death. Our immortal soul will live on and one day be joined together with a body that is driven by God's own Spirit. In addition, since God is the Author of Life, He has complete prerogative over human life. The key to remember here is that God's goal for us is *not physical survival, but enjoying a love relationship with Himself and others.*

"If God cares so much about our souls, then why should we care about the poor?"

Because caring for the poor is what citizens of the reign of God do. The prophets in the Old Testament and Jesus in the New Testament make it clear that God cares very much for the powerless, poor, the orphans, widows, and the outcast. We are to care for them like God cares for them. I can only imagine what He must feel toward us wealthy Americans. This keeps me up at night.

"I still don't think I could believe in a God who didn't stop bad people from doing bad things, or who couldn't stop hurricanes and earthquakes."

God doesn't do illogical things. God can't make a square circle or a married bachelor. In the same vein, God can't create *free-willed* moral agents (humans) and *make them* do something. Remember, if we are to love one another and God, and not just be slaves or robots, we must be free. This same freedom allows evil.

"Go ask a little raped girl if she likes that freedom."

Why? Why does her experience of pain because of someone's evil choice get to be the definitive response to free will? The appropriate response to suffering is grief, not the removal of free will. I absolutely hate rape! I think the person who rapes someone should be punished severely. That is, I think the *person who chose the evil* should be punished, not the capacity of free will.

Just because humans hate evil, and experience pain because of it, doesn't mean free will isn't worth it. Imagine being locked in a room for every day of the week. No one can get in and you can't get out. Every-once-in-a-while, a parent walks by your room. One day you ask your parent, "Can I please get out? Please? I don't want to spend the rest of my life locked in this room." Your parent responds, "Why? You're safe in there. No one can make you suffer. Sure you're not free, but at least you're safe."

What is better: to stay locked up, not able to interact with others, not able to experience free, loving relationships with others, and not able to live where you'd like; or, to be free from that room, free to experience loving relationships, but always at risk for being hurt and hurting others?

"I hear what you're saying. I do. But I still don't like it."

I don't like suffering either. I don't like evil. I *do* like free will.

If you were a Christian, you'd see that while Christians still hate evil, we are certain that God comforts us in our suffering. "God is our refuge and strength, a very present help in trouble" (Psalm 46:1). I can't convince you of this using scientific data. It's something you experience once you join the family of God.

The death of Jesus was in response to the evil humans do. And for those who reject God, hell will be in response to a lifetime of evil done. Hell is real.

"OK. What about hell?"

I don't want to go there.

[Laughs] "Right. Good. But you really think God is moral if He punishes people forever and ever because of some sins they committed?"

Again, I just want to keep us aware that these questions have no bearing whatsoever concerning God's existence, the truth claims of Christianity, or my religious experience. I don't mean any disrespect, but these questions are all peripheral. The existence of hell, even *if* it is an eternity of torture, holds no bearing on anything we've discussed.

"Well, maybe, yes. But I don't want to believe in a God who would do such a thing."

OK. But . . . again . . . I just need to point out that your *desire* not to believe is a moral or psychological choice, not a decision driven by the evidence.

I have a few reflections concerning hell.

First, if God wants to eternally torture rebellious sinners in hell, then that is His prerogative. Really. God has the right, as a perfectly moral Being, to punish immorality in any way that He sees fit. And like I said, this wouldn't make anything we've discussed so far not true. With God, *we get God the way He is,* not the way we might *want* Him to be; just like you can't get *me* in a way that doesn't exist. And if hell is for sinners—which it is—then we *all* deserve it. God has no exterior compulsion to save us.

Secondly, Christians have never reached a consensus concerning the details of hell. Jesus spoke about it several times, so it certainly is a reality, but when He did describe it, He uses different metaphors and images. It can be described as a place of "fire" (which meant judgment to ancient Jews), "outer darkness," being "cast out," or being cast into a "pit." The Greek word for "hell" in English translations is *Gehenna,* which was a physical location, a valley, in Jesus' day. It refers to the burning trash dump outside the city gates of Jerusalem. To be "cast out" into *that* "pit" or "fire" was to be cast out of the community of the faithful. When Jesus describes the people in the "outer darkness" or "fiery furnace" they are "weeping" and "gnashing their teeth" in grief, anger and rebellion (e.g., Matt 8:12; 13:50). He doesn't say they will be "burning alive forever as their skin melts off." Like trash, those in hell are the waste of humanity—no longer useful or welcome into the community of God. And apparently, they will realize their condition.

Now, there's more to the metaphors then I've gone into here, but you can read about it later if you'd like. There are descriptions of people being *destroyed* and there are descriptions of people being *punished forever*. Perhaps both occur. In any case, the descriptions are not scientific: they are poetic descriptions of what it will be like for those who no longer bear the image of God.

"But why is that OK?"

God doesn't *want* people to perish; He wants everyone to repent (2 Peter 3:9). He doesn't get excited to see people be punished (Ezekiel 18:23). God is not salivating, rubbing His hands together, and saying to the angels: "Hot dog! There goes another one! Woot! Hell is more popular than Facebook!"

There are two views of *why* people go to hell, and I would argue that they are complimentary. Hell is a choice of the will *and* a punishment by God. Let me explain both.

On the one hand, hell is a place or state of existence *chosen* by those who reject the love of God. Paul says three times in the beginning of Romans that God's wrath was dished out on the Gentiles by "handing them over" to their own depraved mind. I would argue that hell is like that—that God "hands us over" to our depraved mind in hell. That is, God loves us so much that He respects our free will for as long as we exist. This means that those who reject His love *will continue rejecting it in the next life.* We are becoming the kind of people—now, in this life—that we will become in eternity.

On the other hand, Jesus can speak about hell being punishment for not living a lifestyle of love toward God and neighbor. We can't ever forget that God is perfectly moral. While I don't know what God will do to people in hell, I do believe that He has the moral right to punish people for a life time of breaking the Moral Law. Now, like I said earlier, Christians disagree on whether or not His punishment will last *forever*, or if eventually these people will be destroyed. Like I said, perhaps both are true. There are scripture verses that support both.

So, people will be in hell because God, in his punishment, allowed humans to choose an existence that is utterly devoid of love, forgiveness, and service.

I believe C.S. Lewis expresses it very well: "I willingly believe that the damned are, in one sense, successful, rebels to the end; that the doors of hell are locked on the *inside*. I do not mean that the ghosts may not *wish* to come out of hell, in the vague fashion wherein an envious man 'wishes' to be happy: but they certainly do not will even the first preliminary stages of that self-abandonment through which alone the soul can reach any good. They enjoy forever the horrible freedom they have demanded, and are therefore self-enslaved just as the blessed, forever submitting to obedience, become through all eternity more and more free."[11]

"Why wouldn't God just forgive them?"

Do you see what you're asking? You're asking for something God has *already* offered. He has done that through the death and resurrection of Jesus. That's why Christians are so emphatic on this point: responding to the free gift of God's forgiveness through Jesus is very important!

"Well, I know of some people who will love to be separated from God."

Well, it's unclear how "separate" from God you can be, since you can't go somewhere God is not. Rather, those in hell are certainly separated from God's love.

Gregory Boyd makes the great point that for those who reject God's love, hell seems delightful, but for those who have experienced God's love, hell is "nightmarishly repulsive." "The alcoholic who loves his bottle above his wife, kids, and home has what he wants when they finally 'leave him alone.' But don't the rest of us, who are not that sick, see this as hell? . . . The drunk gets what he wants, but is in hell with this 'privilege.' He is tormented, but it is a torment of his own choosing."[12]

I've heard people say stupid things like, "Hell's gonna' be awesome! I don't have be around God. I can do whatever I wish!" This is pure nonsense. This is worse than saying, "I can't *wait* to be addicted to meth, pawn all I own to buy more of it, live in utter poverty, cut myself off from every friend and family member I have, and overdose on drugs so that I can finally do whatever I wish!" No one in her right mind would desire such a stupid thing.

[Long pause.]

I don't like talking about hell. I don't even like thinking about hell. And I certainly don't want you to miss the point that hell is really, really bad, and you don't have to go there.

[Long pause.]

"So, isn't the Trinity contradictory?"

No. Jews have always believed that there is one God. Yet, when they spoke of God's functions, they could use distinct vocabulary. They spoke of God *the Father* typically as Creator and Sustainer of the cosmos. They typically spoke of God's *presence* and *prophetic voice* as His Spirit. They typically spoke of God's *creating power* and *direction for humans* as God's Wisdom.

So, when Jesus was resurrected and all the pieces were in place, they simply associated God's Wisdom with Jesus. There you have it. God the Father, His Wisdom/Son, and His Spirit.

God is one being with three persons (or centers of consciousness), who all share the exact same essence (or "deityness"). God is *not* three persons in one person or three beings in one being. God is one God. Each person of the Godhead serves a different function. They are not three different gods, like the Greek or Roman gods, but they are all united in essence, will, and love.

"But how can God have three different centers of consciousness? I don't understand that."

God has the capacity to have three rational faculties, or three centers of consciousness. William Lane Craig says it well, I think:

"We naturally equate a rational soul with a person, since the human souls with which we are acquainted are persons. But the reason human souls are individual persons is because each soul is equipped with one set of rational faculties sufficient for being a person. Suppose, then, that God is a soul which is endowed with three complete sets of rational cognitive faculties, each sufficient for personhood. Then God, though one soul, would not be one person but three, for God would have three centers of self-consciousness, intentionality, and volition, as Social Trinitarians maintain. God would clearly not be three discrete souls because the cognitive faculties in question are all faculties belonging to just one soul, one immaterial substance. God would therefore be one being which supports three persons, just as our individual beings each support one person."[13]

There's so much more to it than this, but for now, this will be enough. I'd just like to say again that the Christian idea of God didn't develop by a bunch of dudes in a room talking to each other: "Hey, let's make it complex! They'll think it's true!" No, the belief that God is one being in three persons developed *historically* and *experientially*. They were forced to develop the Trinity in response to what had happened within history. The act preceded the reflection.

Hurtado concurs: "The struggle to work out doctrinal formulations that could express in some coherent way this peculiar view of God (as 'one' and yet somehow comprising 'the Father' and Jesus, thereafter also including the Spirit as the 'third Person' of the Trinity) occupied the best minds in early Christian orthodox/catholic tradition for the first several centuries. But the doctrinal problem they worked on was not of their making. It was forced upon them by the earnest convictions and devotional practice of believers from the earliest observable years of the Christian movement."[14]

"Well, I guess I'll have to take your word for it. What about all those other people in other religions? They sure are passionate about what they believe."

That's right. This is why passion is irrelevant. We determine which religion is true not by comparing who's the most passionate, but by examining the truth claims of each religion. I could be passionately wrong. I could be passionately right. The reasons we have are what makes us right or wrong.

And I know this is very difficult for most Western people to understand. Most Americans I know think that religion isn't *knowledge* or *fact*, but just preference or taste. For most people, talking about which religion you believe in is like talking about which restaurant is your favorite. To say that one religion is "right" is like saying there is only one true restaurant.

But this is nonsense. Religions are based on truth claims. These truth claims are either true or false. We examine them. We think critically about them. This is how we determine which religion is true or not.

"But the only reason you're a Christian is because you were born in America. Had you been born in India you'd be a Hindu."

Perhaps. It *is* more likely that I'd be Hindu if I were born in India. But this doesn't guarantee that I'd be Hindu. If it guaranteed that, then every Indian would be Hindu. But that's not true. There are millions of Christians there. How could that be if the country of origin dictated what I believe? Also, and most importantly, this is called the "genetic fallacy" in logic. You can't determine whether or not something is true by determining *the source of the belief*. Even if I were more likely to be Christian because of America, it doesn't mean Christianity is false. And certainly by now I've demonstrated that I'm not a Christian because of some blind family allegiance.

[Long pause.]

"What would you say to this? I've heard Christopher Hitchens and Sam Harris say that in order to believe in God, you have to believe that He watched our species from 'on High' for at least one hundred thousand years with indifference. And then, for some capricious reason, he decided to reveal Himself to some backwoods, Iron Age Palestinian people. They argue, of course, that it is preposterous to believe such a heinous thing. Imagine being a primitive human, scared at the thunder and wind, and not knowing basic scientific facts. Why would God allow this? Why show up late in human development? This would be profoundly capricious and cruel if it were true."

> The first thing I'd say is that fortunately, the argument, "I don't like what God might or might not have done among primitive humans," is irrelevant. How would Hitchens possibly know what this God-whom-He-doesn't–believe-in-in-the-first-place may or may not have done 100,000 years ago, or what His motivations might have been?
>
> Where is God *right now* when people are scared? My own children still get scared at thunder and the wind. Am I forced to believe that God doesn't exist because my own children are scared of the weather? (Of course, as a Christian, I believe God *is* present now, regardless of how scared we get.)

"Well, I know it's getting late."

> Yep. But I've really enjoyed it!

"Thanks. I must admit: I didn't think you'd have this much to say!"

> [Laughs] Anything else?

"I still have questions."

> I bet! I do too! I also know there are arguments against all that we've discussed. My hope is that at least we've covered some major points for you to consider. Also, go back and read those books I mentioned. Of course, the first books I'd start reading are the Gospels. Read them carefully. Don't give up searching. Based on what the Bible teaches and on my own experience, I'm convinced that those who earnestly seek God will find Him.
>
> And I mean this respectfully, but it's a lot easier to keep asking questions than to finally decide what you will do with the information we've already discussed.

"Hmm . . . I think I remember what you've said. You're a Christian because you think there is scientific evidence that points to God, that Jesus really was resurrected and Christianity is true, and you've had religious experience that confirms it all."

You got it!

"I just feel resistant to all this. I mean, some of this really makes sense, but I feel so resistant."

I know what you mean. Your feeling is not unique. I agree with C.S. Lewis that "before we can be cured we must want to be cured."[15] There must come a time of surrender to the facts and to the person before those feelings of resistance will go away. If you're like me, it might take some time for the intellectual questions to be answered. And I'm very aware that there are tons of other things we haven't discussed. Nevertheless, we've covered enough for you and I to make an informed decision.

"So what did *you* do when after you studied these facts? What I mean is, if someone decided to believe all this, what would the next step be?"

I decided to surrender to the facts that were so compelling. And I realized that I can't love arguments, conclusions, evidence, or facts. I had to move from arguments to a person. Like with my wife, there was only so long that I could resist falling in love! I began talking as if someone was listening. I spoke to God like I would my friend, but with much more fear and reverence. I told God that I was extremely sorry for breaking His Moral Law. I told God that I was very sorry for not loving Him as much as He loved me. I told Him that I was sorry for not loving my neighbor as much as I love myself. I decided to put my trust in Him. I asked Him to forgive me, to come inside me and enable me to be a *real* human. And I received a phenomenal feeling that I was not expecting that affirmed my decision. I committed myself to being a disciple, or student, of Jesus for the rest of my life. I began reading the Bible regularly. I began praying regularly. I joined a church. I made friends with other Christians who encouraged me and held me accountable.

"But even if I decided to do that, there's no way that I could be perfect like Jesus."

That's right! Join the club! "[A] Christian is not a man who never goes wrong, but a man who is enabled to repent and pick himself up and begin over again after each stumble—because the Christ-life is inside him, repairing him all the time, enabling him to repeat (in some degree) the kind of voluntary death which Christ Himself carried out."[16] Christians are not flawless, but they are redeemed. They are Christ's hands and feet, ministering to a hurting and broken world, even though they are also broken. And this can only happen if Jesus does it *for* us and *through* us.

[Long pause.]

"So you don't ever doubt?"

Yes. I do. But there's a difference between what I *know* to be true and my changing moods. I like how Alister McGrath says it:

"*[D]oubt and faith are both states of mind or attitudes.* Doubt can be a constant attitude of questioning toward God, where faith can be a constant attitude of trust and openness. We are being asked to develop a permanent attitude of openness and trust toward God—not just to be open to him and trust him on any one occasion, but to be like this all the time. This results in conflict at times, since our old tendency to doubt God surfaces, but this just underscores out need to commit ourselves more fully to him again."[17]

We can't ignore our feelings, but we can't base what we believe on them either. They change too much. As C.S. Lewis said, "Feelings come and go, and when they come a good use can be made of them: they cannot be our regular spiritual diet."[18] So, again, feelings do matter, but we just have to remember that feelings can betray us. I know for a fact that my dentist will not stab me with that little, evil

177

drill. Nevertheless, my anxiety skyrockets every time I hear that high-pitched noise. My feelings would convince me that I'm in danger. I have to sit in the chair and say over and over again, "No. Calm down. You're not in danger. She knows what she's doing. Trust her."[19]

"That's true! I do that too at the dentist!"

I do the same with my feelings toward God. I tell my feelings to calm down when necessary. When I doubt, I go back to what I know is true based on the facts we've discussed.

[Long pause.]

I do know that God invites us into a love relationship. He does give us a "stirring in our spirit" that feels like excitement. Our heart races and our mind imagines, "Is it true?" But it's up to you to respond. God won't force Himself upon you. If He were to do that, you couldn't love Him in return freely.

I appreciate how Gregory Boyd says it: "[F]aith is more than a historical hypothesis. It is also a decision: a moral decision. The question is not only, 'Do you rationally see why you should believe?' but also 'Do you want to believe?'" There's plenty of solid evidence for anyone who wants to believe, but enough faith is required to still render it a moral choice and not a coerced decision. God desires faith because He seeks love from responsible people, not forced behavior from robots."[20]

So what do you think?

As the great fourth-century bishop, Gregory of Nyssa, said, "If a man in broad daylight of his own free will closes his eyes, the sun is not responsible for his failure to see."[21]

So, I'm curious: after all we've talked about . . . are your eyes closed, or are you choosing to see?

Reflection Questions

(Primarily for those who believe in God)

Preface

1. If you believe in God, have you ever seriously considered how you are viewed by those who don't believe in God? Do you think it would help you dialogue with Materialists if you seriously considered *their point of view?*

Chapter One:

Are you really open-minded?

1. When someone asks you a question (such as, "Couldn't you be delusional?"), do you think it's helpful or not helpful to admit that we *might be?*

2. The author lists three main reasons why He believes in the Christian God. What are they? Would you say the same? If not, what would your primary reasons be?

3. Do you believe in any other gods? If not, could you tell someone *why* you don't believe in them?

4. What is the point of the analogy of the *a*-brotherist?

5. Notice the tone and attitude of the skeptic. What are some ways to "keep your cool" when someone speaks with disdain?

Chapter Two:

It's all about worldview

1. What is Materialism? Scientism? Logical Positivism? Can you give some names of persons who represent these ideas? Why are these views false?

2. Could you list the six examples of facts of the universe that are

not made of matter or energy and cannot be proven by science? What does this demonstrate?

3. Can you demonstrate or prove a negative assertion?

4. The author gives seven possible reasons why a person would reject belief in God. Do you agree or disagree? Would you take away or add any reasons? Do you have any emotional or psychological reasons for believing *in* God?

5. How does your worldview affect the way you come to conclusions about God?

Chapter Three:

Scientific evidence for God and the meaning of "belief"

1. What does this author suggest is the reason why God doesn't perform miracles all the time? Why doesn't He write a message in the sky?

2. The author says that there is one type of evidence that could never be given for God. What is it?

3. What is the point of the analogy of the painter?

4. The author says that basing belief in God on science is misplaced and dangerous. Why?

5. According to the author, how should we use the word "believe" and "prove" when we speak about God? Do you agree or disagree?

Chapter Four:

Scientific facts that point to God: The origin of the universe

1. The author suggests that no one can prove God exists. What does he mean by that? Do you agree or disagree?

2. What are the five (or six) scientific facts that the author believes points to God? Would you add or subtract from these?

3. What does the origin of the universe imply about God? Why can't gravity create the universe?

4. What did this author say in response to the question, "Then who created God?"

Chapter Five:

Scientific facts that point to God: The universe knew we were coming

1. What does the design of the universe imply about God?
2. What's the gambler's fallacy?
3. What does the firing squad analogy demonstrate?
4. What is the point of the analogy of the baby crib and tree swing?
5. What is the point of the analogy of the village and the dam?

Chapter Six:

Scientific facts that point to God: The origin of life

1. Why is it so unlikely that life began by non-rational, natural processes?
2. DNA/RNA implies what? Why is this important?
3. What is the point of the analogy John Lennox gives concerning the person who finds the car factory?

Chapter Seven:

More facts that point to God: morality and the soul

1. What is the evidence for a Moral Law? What does a Moral Law imply?
2. Why can't morality come from evolution?
3. How is the Moral Law like the laws of mathematics?
4. Where does the Moral Law come from?
5. How does the author define a soul? What are the three evidences the author gives for the soul?

Chapter Eight:

Why I believe Jesus was deity

1. If someone argues that Bart Ehrman has recently demonstrated that the New Testament documents can't be trusted, what would you say?

2. What's the significance of understanding the Gospels as *ancient* biographies?

3. Why didn't Jesus say, "I'm God"?

4. What are six implicit things concerning Jesus that would have convinced any first-century Jew that Jesus was deity?

5. Why can't we just argue that Jesus was simply a great moral teacher?

6. What are some changes that the primitive Jewish-Christians did that demonstrated they believed Jesus was deity?

Chapter Nine:

Why I believe Jesus was resurrected

1. What does resurrection mean? For the Jews who believed in resurrection, what did they believe about it? How were Christians different?

2. What are the five independent sources for the resurrection? Which is the earliest?

3. Why is it very probable that the Gospels contain primitive accounts of the resurrection?

4. The primitive Jewish-Christians had radical changes in their beliefs and practices after the resurrection. What were those changes?

5. What is the point of the analogy of soccer?

6. Why is the ministry and death of Jesus significant?

Chapter Ten:

Why I believe I've met the Spirit of the risen Jesus

1. Why does the author argue that religious experience is important. Do you agree or disagree?

2. What are the reasons given for believing that the author had a *religious* experience, and not just an emotional experience?

3. Have you had religious experiences with God? If so, how would you explain this?

Chapter Eleven:

Odds and ends

1. Why is it irrelevant if God doesn't answer every prayer?

2. Does God intend that humans be pain-free and happy all the time? If not, why not? What is God's goal for humans?

3. Why is their evil? Why is their suffering?

4. What is the genetic fallacy? Why does it matter in the discussion of belief in God?

5. The author listed several common questions for Christians in this chapter. What are some other questions you've heard posed to Christians? What are concise answers to those questions?

6. Is it OK to doubt? Why do we doubt? What do we do if we doubt God or our faith?

Endnotes

Preface

[1]   C.S. Lewis, *Mere Christianity* (New York: Touchstone, 1980), 41.

Chapter One

Are you really open-minded?

[1]   For a similar list, see Norman Geisler and Frank Turek, *I Don't Have Enough Faith to be Atheist*, (Wheaton: Crossway Books, 2004), 165-166.

[2]   From "Billions and Billions of Demons," a book review in *The New York Review of Books*, Jan 9, 1997 concerning Carl Sagan's book, *The Demon-Haunted World: Science as a Candle in the Dark* (http://www.nybooks.com/articles/archives/1997/jan/09/billions-and-billions-of-demons/) (Accessed 5/21/11).

[3]   Francis Collins, *The Language of God: A Scientist Presents Evidence for Belief* (New York: Free Press, 2006), 20, 21.

[4]   Italics mine. http://www.time.com/time/magazine/article/0,9171,1555132-5,00.html#ixzz1MzylmOHg (Accessed 5/21/11).

[5]   Augustine, "On Genesis: A Refutation of the Manichees, II, 3," in *On Genesis*, trans. By Edmund Hill (New York: New City Press, 2002), 72.

Chapter Two

It's all about worldview

[1]   Peter Atkins, in John Corwell, ed., *Nature's Imagination – The Frontiers of Scientific Vision* (Oxford, Oxford University Press, 1995), 125.

[2]   http://hyperphysics.phy-astr.gsu.edu/nave-html/faithpathh/Russell.html (accessed 9/25/11)

[3]   Roy Abraham Varghese, "Preface," in Antony Flew and Roy Abraham Varghese, *There is a God* (Kindle Edition, 2009), Location 177.

[4]   Antony Flew and Roy Abraham Varghese, *There is a God*, Location 1111.

5   Einstein, *The Quotable Einstein*, ed. Alice Calaprice (Princeton, NJ: Princeton University Press, 2005), 238, found in Roy Abraham Varghese, "Preface," *There is a God*, Location 228.

6   Ian H. Hutchinson, "Engaging Today's Militant Atheist Arguments," from The BioLogos Foundation (www.BioLogos.org/projects/scholar-essays), 4-5.

7   Stephen Hawking and Leonard Mlodinow, *The Grand Design* (New York: Bantam, 2010), 5.

8   John Lennox makes this point often in presentations, debates, and books. I don't recall where I heard it first.

9   Ian H. Hutchinson, "Engaging Today's Militant Atheist Arguments," 5.

10   These come from William Lane Craig. I first saw it on http://www.youtube.com/watch?v=gkBD2oedOco, but it's also in Norman Geisler and Frank Turek, *I Don't Have Enough Faith to be an Atheist*, 126-127.

11   C.S. Lewis, *Miracles: A Preliminary Study* (HarperCollins, New York: 1947; renewed 1996), 43.

12   William Lane Craig, *On Guard: Defending Your Faith with Reason and Precision* (David C. Cook Publisher, 2010; Kindle Location 2403).

13   C.S. Lewis, "On Obstinacy in Belief," in *The World's Last Night and Other Essays* (Harcourt, Inc.; New York, 1952; renewed 1987), 18.

14   Heard on the video, "Duelling Professors (John Lennox vs. Peter Atkins); http://www.youtube.com/watch?v=YxoCXmagQuo (Accessed on 5/15/11).

15   John Loftus, *Why I Became an Atheist: A Former Preacher Rejects Christianity* (Prometheus Books, 2008).

16   Paul Vitz, *Faith of the Fatherless: The Psychology of Atheism* (Spence Publishing Co., 2000).

17   John Lennox, *God's Undertaker: Has Science Buried God?* (Kindle Edition, 2009), Location 887.

18   http://www.ignatiusinsight.com/features2005/jbudziszewski_int1_feb05.asp (Accessed 6/23/22).

19   J. Budziszewski, "Why I Am Not an Atheist," in Norman Geisler and Paul Hoffman, eds., *Why I Am a Christian: Leading Thinkers Explain Why They Believe* (Grand Rapids: baker, 2001), 54.

20   Alister McGrath makes the same point in *Doubting* (Downers Grove: InterVarsity Press, 2006), 35.

21   C.S. Lewis, "On Obstinacy in Belief," 19.

22   C.S. Lewis, "On Obstinacy in Belief," 19.

Chapter Three

Scientific evidence for God and the meaning of "belief"

1   Alister McGrath, *Doubting* (Downers Grove: InterVarsity Press, 2006), 25.

2   Gregory A. Boyd and Edward K. Boyd, *Letters from a Skeptic* (Colorado Springs: Life Journey, 2004),123.

3   Francis Collins, *The Language of God: A Scientist Presents Evidence for Belief* (New York: Free Press, 2006), 30.

4   Richard Dawkins, *The God Delusion* (London: Bantam, 2006), 58-59; Roy Abraham, "Preface," in Antony Flew and Roy Varghese, *There is a God* (Kindle Edition, 2009), Location 177.

5   Alister McGrath, *The Passionate Intellect: Christian Faith and the Discipleship of the Mind* (IVP: Downers Grove, 2010), 110.

6   http://en.wikipedia.org/wiki/Yuri_Gagarin#Space_flight (Accessed 5/21/11).

7   McGrath, *The Passionate Intellect*, 110.

8   Found in Martin H. Manser, *The Westminster collection of Christian quotations* (Louisville: John Knox Press, 2001), 132.

9   Francis Collins, *The Language of God*, 93.

10   C.S. Lewis, "On Obstinacy in Belief," in *The World's Last Night and Other Essays* (Harcourt, Inc.; New York, 1952; renewed 1987), 16.

11   C.S. Lewis, "On Obstinacy in Belief," 17.

12   Richard Dawkins, "Is Science a Religion?" in Louis Pojman and Michael Rea, *Philosophy of Religion: An Anthology* (Belmont: Thomson higher Education, 2008), 426.

13   David Wood, "Responding the Problem of Evil," in Michael Licona and William A. Dembski, *Evidence for God: 50 Arguments for Faith from the Bible, History, Philosophy, and Science* (Kindle Edition), 38.

14   Alister McGrath, *Doubting*, 25.

15   C.S. Lewis, *Mere Christianity* (New York: HarperCollins: 1952, 1980), 140.

16   C.S. Lewis, "On Obstinacy in Belief," 17.

17   C.S. Lewis, "On Obstinacy in Belief," 16.

18   Dawkins, "Is Science a Religion?", 426.

19   C.S. Lewis, "On Obstinacy in Belief," 20, italics mine.

20   C.S. Lewis, "On Obstinacy in Belief," 21-22.

21   Francis Collins, *The Language of God*, 58.

22   C.S. Lewis, "On Obstinacy in Belief," 22.

23   C.S. Lewis, "On Obstinacy in Belief," 26.

24   C.S. Lewis, "On Obstinacy in Belief," 28.

Chapter Four

Scientific facts that point to God: The origin of the universe

1   C.S. Lewis, *Miracles: A Preliminary Study* (New York: HarperCollins, 1947; restored 1996), 169.

2   http://abcnews.go.com/WN/Technology/stephen-hawking-religion-science-win/story?id=10830164 (Accessed 5/3/11).

3   Found in Francis Collins, *The Language of God: A Scientist Presents Evidence for Belief* (New York: Free Press, 2006), 165-166.

4   Stephen Hawking and Roger Penrose, *The Nature of Space and Time*, The Isaac Newton Institute Series of Lectures (Princeton: Princeton University Press, 1996), 20; in William Lane Craig and J.P. Moreland, *Philosophical Foundations for a Christian Worldview* (Downers Grove, Ill: InterVarsity Press, 2003), 478.

5   William Lane Craig, *Reasonable Faith*, 3rd Ed. (Wheaton: Crossway, 2008), 165.

6   C.S. Lewis, *Mere Christianity* (New York: Touchstone, 1980), 32.

7   William Lane Craig, *Reasonable Faith*, 154.

8   Hawking and Mlodinow, "Why God Did Not Create the Universe," *The Wall Street Journal*, 9/3/2010.

9   The same point, and the following critique, is also made in John Lennox, *God and Stephen Hawking* (Lion Books, 2011).

10   Roy Abraham Varghese, "New Atheism": A Critical Appraisal of Dawkins, Dennett, Wolpert, Harris, and Stenger," in Antony Flew and Roy Abraham Varghese, *There is a God* (Kindle Edition, 2009), Location 1755.

11   This is a common critique. For example, Roy Abraham Varghese, "New Atheism," Location 1849.

12   For this discussion, see Chapter Three in William Lane Craig, *On Guard*,

especially Kindle Locations, 919-920.

13 http://www.time.com/time/magazine/article/0,9171,1555132-5,00.html
#ixzz1No65ynva

14 http://www.time.com/time/magazine/article/0,9171,1555132-6,00.html
#ixzz1No5soaAh

15 Richard Dawkins go even farther. He states that believing in a Creator God
"does seem to me to be a worthy idea. Refutable—but nevertheless grand
and big enough to be worthy of respect." Yet, this is as far as he'll go. As
he states often, the belief that the Creator God came to Earth in any form
is simple-minded, petty, and parochial. See http://www.time.com/time/
magazine/article/0,9171,1555132-9,00.html#ixzz1No7ymW6H.

16 David Beck, "The Cosmological Argument," in Michael Licona and William
A. Dembski, *Evidence for God: 50 Arguments for Faith from the Bible,
History, Philosophy, and Science* (Kindle Edition), 16.

17 This kind of statement was made by Christopher Hitchens often in his
debates.

Chapter Five

Scientific facts that point to God:

The universe knew we were coming

1 http://www.reasons.org/fine-tuning-life-universe (Accessed on 6/22/11).

2 John C. Lennox, *God's Undertaker: Has Science Buried God?* (Kindle Edition),
70.

3 Hugh Ross, "Why I Believe in the Miracle of Divine Creation," in Norman
Geisler and Paul Hoffman, eds., *Why I Am a Christian: Leading Thinkers
Explain Why They Believe* (Grand Rapids: baker, 2001), 143-44.

4 http://en.wikipedia.org/wiki/Fred_Hoyle (Accessed on 5/25/11).

5 Fred Hoyle, "The Universe: Past and Present Reflections," *Engineering and
Science* (November 1981): 8–12.

6 http://www.cosmicfingerprints.com/hugh-ross-origin-of-the-universe/
(Accessed on 11/14/2011).

7 William Lane Craig, *Reasonable Faith*, 3rd Ed. (Wheaton: Crossway, 2008),
165.

8 This is a similar charge that Richard Dawkins makes: http://www.time.com/
time/magazine/article/0,9171,1555132-5,00.html#ixzz1No65ynva

9   John C. Polkinghorne, *One World: The Interaction of Science and Theoloy* (London: SPCK, 1986), 80; John C. Lennox, *God's Undertaker* (Kindle Edition), 74-75.

10   http://www.reasons.org/infinity-universes-0 (Accessed on 12/3/2011).

11   http://abcnews.go.com/WN/Technology/stephen-hawking-religion-science-win/story?id=10830164 (Accessed on 5/28/11).

12   See William Lane Craig, *On Guard*, Chapter Two: "What Difference Does it Make if God Exists?".

13   This question (Why should I care about the long term?) was asked in a different form by the Yale philosopher Shelley Kagan. William Lane Craig gave a similar response to this one in a debate sponsored by the Veritas Forum. See http://www.youtube.com/watch?v=ZzlXz Cz9Jgl&feature=related.

14   http://abcnews.go.com/WN/Technology/stephen-hawking-religion-science-win/story?id=10830164 (Accessed on 6/24/11).

Chapter Six

Scientific facts that point to God: The origin of life

1   The following five reasons are from Walter Bradley, "The Origin of Life," in *Evidence for God: 50 Arguments for Faith from the Bible, History, Philosophy, and Science* Michael Licona and William A. Dembski, (Kindle Edition), 64-67.

2   Walter Bradley, "The Origin of Life," 66.

3   Steven Meyer, *Signature in the Cell: DNA and the Evidence for Intelligent Design* (New York: HarperCollins, 2009), 212.

4   Walter Bradley, "The Origin of Life," 65-66.

5   Walter Bradley, "The Origin of Life," 67.

6   Richard Dawkins, *The Blind Watchmaker* (New York: Norton, 1987), 17-18, 116, in Norman Geisler and Frank Turek, *I Don't Have Enough Faith to be Atheist* (Wheaton: Crossway Books, 2004), 116.

7   Francis Collins, *The Language of God: A Scientist Presents Evidence for Belief* (New York: Free Press, 2006), 92-93.

8   Francis Collins, *The Language of God*, 93.

9   I'm uncertain if I developed this analogy or if I heard this first from John Lennox. If it is from John Lennox, I can't recall the reference (a debate, perhaps?).

10   William Lane Craig, *Contending with Christianity's Critics: Answering New Atheists and Other Objectors* (Kindle Edition, 2009), 4-5.

11   Hugh Ross, "Why I Believe in the Miracle of Divine Creation," 146.

12   John C. Lennox, *God's Undertaker: Has Science Buried God?* (Kindle Edition), 91.

13   Steven J. Gould, Paul McGarr, and *et al.*, *The Richness of Life: the Essential* (2007), 263.

Chapter Seven

More facts that point to God: morality and the soul

1   C.S. Lewis, *Mere Christianity* (New York: HarperCollins: 1952, 1980), 33.

2   A similar point is made in William Lane Craig, *On Guard: Defending Your Faith with Reason and Precision* (David C. Cook Publisher, 2010), Kindle Location 2136.

3   Francis Collins, *The Language of God: A Scientist Presents Evidence for Belief* (New York: Free Press, 2006), 23.

4   C.S. Lewis, *Mere Christianity*, 23.

5   C.S. Lewis, *Mere Christianity*, 24.

6   Paul Copan, "The Moral Argument for God's Existence," in Michael Licona and William A. Dembski, *Evidence for God: 50 Arguments for Faith from the Bible, History, Philosophy, and Science* (Kindle Edition), 23.

7   C.S. Lewis, *Miracles: A Preliminary Study* (New York: HarperCollins, 1947; restored 1996), 51.

8   Richard Dawkins, *The Selfish Gene*, 3rd ed. (Oxford Press, 2006), 3.

9   Antony Flew and Roy Abraham Varghese, *There is a God* (Kindle Edition, 2009), Location 1031.

10   Antony Flew and Roy Abraham Varghese, *There is a God*, Location 1034.

11   Roy Abraham Varghese, Roy Abraham Varghese, "New Atheism": A Critical Appraisal of Dawkins, Dennett, Wolpert, Harris, and Stenger," in Antony Flew and Roy Abraham Varghese, *There is a God* (Kindle Edition, 2009), Location 1887.

12   Roy Abraham Varghese, "New Atheism," Location 1887.

13   Roy Abraham Varghese, "New Atheism," Location 1992.

14   C.S. Lewis, *Miracles*, 41.

15 C.S. Lewis, *Miracles*, 40.

16 C.S. Lewis, *Miracles*, 62.

17 Jeffery Long, with Paul Perry, *Evidence of the Afterlife: The Science of Near Death Experiences* (Kindle Edition, 2009), Location 734.

18 Jeffery Long, with Paul Perry, *Evidence of the Afterlife*, Location 1843.

19 Karl Popper and John Eccles, *The Self and Its Brain* (New York: Springer-Verlag, 1977), 559-60; found in David Wood, "God, Suffering, and Santa Claus: An Examination of the Explanatory Power of Theism and Atheism," in Michael Licona and William A. Dembski, (Kindle Edition), 45.

20 Augustine, "On Genesis: A Refutation of the Manichees, II, 11," in *On Genesis*, 78.

21 Augustine, *The Literal Meaning of Genesis*, esp. X, 17 and 39.

22 Augustine, *The Literal Meaning of Genesis*, X, 39, in *On Genesis*, trans. By Edmund Hill (New York: New City Press, 2002), 423.

Chapter Eight

Why I believe Jesus was deity

1 C.S. Lewis, *Miracles: A Preliminary Study* (New York: HarperCollins, 1947; restored 1996), 173.

2 C.S. Lewis, *Miracles*, 108-109.

3 Found in F.F. Bruce, *The New Testament Documents: Are They Reliable?* 5th Ed. (Downers Grove: InterVarsity Press, 2000), 20.

4 For example, see Ben Witherington, III's detailed critique: http://www.patheos.com/community/bibleandculture/2011/04/06/forged-chapter-three%E2%80%94an-appalling-numerber-of-forgeries/.

5 http://www.gregboyd.org/qa/bible/how-do-you-respond-to-ehrmans-book-misquoting-jesus/ (Accessed on 11/15/2011).

6 This point was also made recently by Dan Wallace in his debate with Bart Ehrman at SMU. The debate was called, "Can We Trust the Text of the New Testament?" on September 1, 2011.

7 F.F. Bruce, *The New Testament Documents: Are They Reliable?* 15.

8 It's typical to appeal to the Gospel of John at this point. However, John's Gospel has proved to be a highly precarious document among historians when attempting to determine what the historical Jesus said.

9   Also see Norman Geisler and Frank Turek, *I Don't Have Enough Faith to be Atheist* (Wheaton: Crossway Books, 2004), 342-345.

10 Larry Hurtado, *Lord Jesus Christ: Devotion to Jesus in Earliest Christianity* (Grand Rapids: Wm. B. Eerdmans, 2005), 641.

11 For the following, also see Larry Hurtado, *Lord Jesus Christ: Devotion to Jesus in Earliest Christianity*, and Norman Geisler and Frank Turek, *I Don't Have Enough Faith to be an Atheist*, 342-345.

12 Larry Hurtado, *Lord Jesus Christ*, 215.

13 Larry Hurtado, *Lord Jesus Christ*, 216.

14 "Narrated Abu Huraira: I heard Allah's Apostle saying. 'By Allah! I ask for forgiveness from Allah and turn to Him in repentance more than seventy times a day.'" Hadith, Sahih Bukhari (Invocations, Volume 8, Book 75, Number 319) (Accessed on http://www.searchtruth.com/book_display. php?book=75&translator=1).

15 Larry Hurtado, *Lord Jesus Christ*, 650.

16 C.S. Lewis, *Mere Christianity*, 54-55.

17 At one point, either the crowd or Jesus' family thought he was "out of his mind" (the antecedent of the verb is unclear) in Mark 3:21.

18 Mark 3:22.

19 C.S. Lewis, *The Joyful Christian* (New York: Touchstone, 1977), 74.

20 http://www.ignatiusinsight.com/features2005/jbudziszewski_int1_feb05. asp (Accessed on 6/23/11).

Chapter Nine

Why I believe Jesus was resurrected

1   N.T. Wright, *The Resurrection of the Son of God* (Christian Origins and the Search for God, Vol. 3; Minneapolis: Fortress Press, 2003), 82-83. See pages 85-206 for Jewish expectations of resurrection.

2   For the following points of how the early Christians spoke of Jesus' resurrection in distinction from their Jewish neighbors, see N.T. Wright, *The Resurrection of the Son of God*, 476-479.

3   N.T. Wright, *Simply Christian: Why Christianity Makes Sense* (New York: HarperCollins, 2003), 113.

4   N.T. Wright, *The Resurrection of the Son of God*, 599-608.

5   N.T. Wright, *Simply Christian*, 112.

6   N.T. Wright, *Simply Christian*, 113.

7   For a similar account of how radically things changed, see Norman Geisler and Frank Turek, *I Don't Have Enough Faith to be an Atheist* (Wheaton: Crossway Books, 2004), 318-319.

8   N.T. Wright, *Simply Christian*, 113.

9   N.T. Wright, *Simply Christian*, 115.

10   N.T. Wright, *Simply Christian*, 111.

11   N.T. Wright, *The Challenge of Jesus* (London: SPCK, 2000), 69.

Chapter Ten

Why I believe I've met the Spirit of the risen Jesus

1   1 John 4:1; 1 Thess 5:21; 2 Cor. 13:5.

2   http://sfy.ru/?script=contact (Accessed on 7/10/11).

Chapter Eleven

Odds and ends

1   C.S. Lewis, "The Efficacy of Prayer," in *The World's Last Night and Other Essays* (Harcourt, Inc.; New York, 1952; renewed 1987), 3.

2   C.S. Lewis, "The Efficacy of Prayer," 4.

3   C.S. Lewis, "The Efficacy of Prayer," 9.

4   N.T. Wright, *Simply Christian: Why Christianity Makes Sense* (New York: HarperCollins, 2003), 111.

5   http://www.cosmicfingerprints.com/hugh-ross-origin-of-the-universe/ (Accessed on 11/15/2011).

6   Dr. Jeff Halverson: http://www.nasa.gov/mission_pages/hurricanes/multimedia/AtlanticHurricanesWithJeffPage7.html (Accessed on 11/17/2011).

7   In this article, the authors argue that a particular kind of bird highly benefits from the effects of hurricanes (http://myweb.fsu.edu/jelsner/PDF/Research/ConvertinoEtAl2011.pdf).

8   http://www.generousgiving.org/stats# (Accessed 11/23/2011).

9   http://www.usatoday.com/tech/news/2011-06-14-entertainment-spending-rises_n.htm (Accessed on 11/23/2011).

10 "The Potential for Funding the Harvest" http://www.generousgiving.org/stats# (Accessed 11/23/11).

11 C.S. Lewis, *The Problem of Pain* (New York: HarperCollins, 1940; renewed 1996), 130.

12 Gregory A. Boyd and Edward K. Boyd, *Letters from a Skeptic* (Colorado Springs: Life Journey, 2004), 163.

13 Found in his essay, "A Formulation and Defense of the Doctrine of the Trinity" (http://www.reasonablefaith.org/site/News2?page=NewsArticle &id=5909; accessed on 12/3/2011).

14 Larry Hurtado, *Lord Jesus Christ: Devotion to Jesus in Earliest Christianity* (Grand Rapids: Wm. B. Eerdmans, 2005), 651.

15 C.S. Lewis, *Mere Christianity* (New York: HarperCollins: 1952, 1980), 93.

16 C.S. Lewis, *Mere Christianity*, 64.

17 Alister McGrath, *Doubting* (Downers Grove: InterVarsity Press, 2006), 53.

18 C.S. Lewis, "The World's Last Night," in *The World's Last Night and Other Essays* (Harcourt, Inc.; New York, 1952; renewed 1987), 109.

19 C.S. Lewis gives a similar analogy in *Mere Christianity*, 139.

20 Gregory A. Boyd and Edward K. Boyd, *Letters from a Skeptic*, 125.

21 Gregory of Nyssa, *Address on Religious Instruction* 7, in Edward R. Hardy, ed., *Christology of the Later Fathers* (Louisville: Westminster Jon Knox Press, 1954), 282.

לֹא לָנוּ יְהוָה לֹא לָנוּ כִּי־לְשִׁמְךָ תֵּן כָּבוֹד
עַל־חַסְדְּךָ עַל־אֲמִתֶּךָ:

Psalm 115:1